FROM THE
ORANGE MAILBOX
Notes From A Few Country Acres

FROM THE ORANGE MAILBOX

Notes From A Few Country Acres

A. CARMAN CLARK

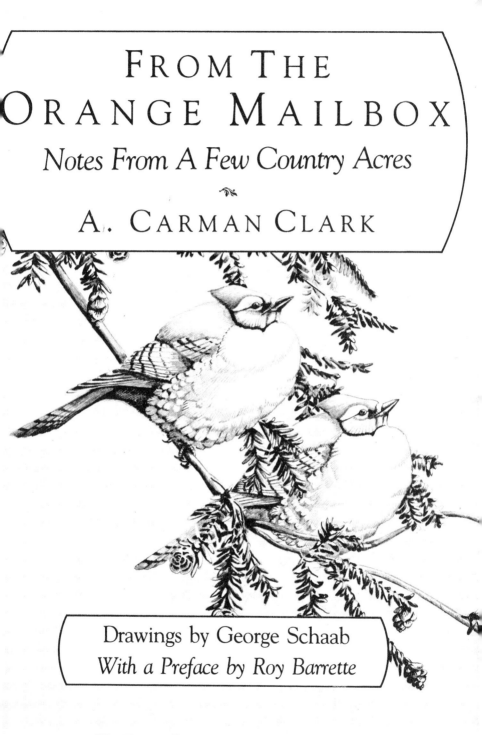

Drawings by George Schaab
With a Preface by Roy Barrette

The Harpswell Press   Gardiner, Maine

Library of Congress Catalog Card Number: 85-45024

ISBN: 0-88448-033-X Cloth
      0-88448-034-8 Paper

Grateful acknowledgement is made to William S. Patten, Publisher of
the *Camden Herald*, where most of the columns in this book were
originally printed.

Asparagus & Rhubarb: Reprinted by permission from *Blair & Ketchum's
COUNTRY JOURNAL*. Copyright © April, 1977 and May, 1977.

Designed on Crummett Mountain by Edith Allard

FIRST EDITION

The Harpswell Press
132 Water Street
Gardiner, Maine 04345

Manufactured in the United States of America

Library of Congress Cataloging-in-Publication Data

Clark, A. Carman, 1917-
   From the orange mailbox.

   1. Country life — Maine — Union Region — Addresses,
essays, lectures. 2. Clark, A. Carman, 1917-   Addresses,
essays, lectures. I. Title.
S521.5.M2C57 1985   974.1'53   85-45024
ISBN 0-88448-033-X
ISBN 0-88448-034-8 (pbk.)

TO JANE GILLIAT FRY
Friend, fellow writer, and honest critic

PREFACE

The English poet, William Blake, who wrote:
"To see the world in a grain of sand
And heaven in a wild flower,
(to) Hold infinity in the palm of your hand
And eternity in an hour . . ."
describes the qualities required of a poet, or an essayist, who is a poet in prose. The one and the other live under the urgency of making visible beauty that has always been there but remained unseen until they bring it into focus.

In one of her columns Arley Clark wrote: "My world is wet and windy. The flooded east field looks like a farm pond where gusts roil the surface as though fish were feeding there." As I read, there came to my mind, a shallow stretch of water behind a broken dam near Seven Ponds stream in the Rangeley district of Maine. My map, an old one, had shown a pond and, like all fishermen, I had sought it as a place, private and unfished for years, where I might land the prize trout. When I reached it there *was* an acre or so of water but it was no more than a couple of feet deep. In disappointment I skimmed a stone across it and its surface broke into a fury of fleeing minnows. I had not thought of it for years until Arley Clark's description of wind ruffling her flooded meadow awakened my memory.

An essayist paints in little, like a miniaturist, but instead of colour, painstakingly applied under a magnifying glass, uses words to accomplish the task. The method, though, is the same. What is needed is a keen eye, a mind that is receptive to every nuance as light as a butterfly's wing, infinite patience and a mastery of the technicalities of the medium.

If you are like me you will enjoy this book. You will not find genius in every line but, if you read quietly with a pencil in your hand, you will discover, or rediscover, things that will put a spark to your memory. You will find you are reminded, suddenly, of a felicitous moment in your past that will bring a smile of happiness to your lips.

Arley Clark deals with the small things of life. The things that constitute all but the tiniest fraction of our experiences.

Roy Barrette

INTRODUCTION

I wrote my first book, a love story, when I was ten years old. A British Lord sailed off to the Land of the Midnight Sun with his beautiful, dying daughter. The cold, clean air of the mountains and the love of a handsome Norwegian restored the fair maiden's health and they lived happily ever after in a stone castle looking west across the Atlantic. That book was never published.

In recent years another kind of love story has brought positive responses from editors. I didn't sail off to Norway to find a cure for my illnesses, to find ways to deal with the frightening echoes of the voice within which kept repeating, "There must be more to life than this." Here on my own hill top, I came to a complete halt long enough to shift from the race to earn a living to forward steps in learning to live. Here in my own back yard, digging in the earth gave me new energy and stirred my curiosity. The multiplying questions helped crowd out self-pity and stagnation, gave birth to a passion for planting, and centered my thoughts on the power behind all growth.

My journals and research turned into magazine articles. Sharing experiences in caring for the land and moving in a new satisfying rhythm with the seasons led to a newspaper column on country living. Each step forward found new doors opening. But first it was necessary to close other doors, move away from the expectations of others, and take full responsibility for my own life.

When my divorce, complicated by a serious illness, left me feeling like a withered turnip, I was glad to find that the viability of the human spirit is rather like that of weeds. Some days, some weeks I reacted like milk weed which, however trampled, broken, or cut down, takes strength from buried roots and grows again—more vulnerable but determined to blossom.

No matter how destructive the relationship may have been for both individuals, divorce is a loss—a kind of death. Hopes and expectations are gone. A commitment made in love and faith is shattered. No matter how right the feeling of freedom and solitude may be, the emotional bankruptcy resulting from failure after an investment of years of living must be faced and worked through before firm steps in building a new life can be undertaken.

Letting go of the feeling that through too many years I had "sold out" by doing what others expected of me—or what I thought they expected—became easier as my physical activity increased. Regular digging and hauling increased my energy and watching the miracles of great green plants growing from tiny, dry seeds stirred my curiosity. I saw my land as a textbook waiting to be studied. Moving on became an adventure.

Originally this farm was 200 acres stretching from the shores of a fresh water pond to the crest of the ridge on the east. During the Civil War 30 acres of woodland was sold but the other 170 acres were almost all cleared for pasture and hay fields. During the last 70 years the acres east of the town road, which runs north and south through the farm, were allowed to grow into woods of pine, hemlock, and birch. Only about 15 acres are now cleared land east of the house.

From the farmhouse on this hilltop, the valley can be viewed with the pond widening to one mile and extending north for almost three miles. I like to believe that the Indians, coming down the St. George River on their way to the coast, used this hill as their sighting mark when they paddled out into open water.

From this hilltop I watch the seasonal cycles. Here I lift

my eyes to the hills and walk beside the water learning the inter-relationships of all the life upon these acres. Here I kneel in the earth and know that the force of life in my gardens, like the sunrises and sunsets, is controlled by a power which will go on long after my life span has ended.

A passion for gardening and an unending curiosity to know more about the soil and all the life upon my acres have made the process of living an adventure I share through writing. Shifting my living patterns and gaining an "alive aloneness" have rewarded me with joy in living each day fully—as though that might be all the time there is. I can't change yesterday and I may not awaken tomorrow morning. But this day is mine.

FROM THE ORANGE MAILBOX
Notes From A Few Country Acres

MARCH

"MY MAILBOX is a doorway to the world." Those words introduced the first Orange Mailbox column in 1982. Research, writing and responding to readers have widened my world.

The idea of writing a column on country living was incubated during the years of being part of *Farm Journal* Family Test Group. The 500 families in this group represented different kinds of farming operations and varied geographical locations throughout the United States. Products were tried and evaluated for the "Use-tested and Approved" seal. Ideas for articles being planned for the 3,000,000 subscribers *Farm Journal* had at that time were sent out to test-group families and we acted as editorial sounding boards. We were encouraged to submit alternatives—new ideas or suggestions for a fresh focus.

When a questionnaire arrived in the mailbox, a response was sent back within twenty-four hours. Usually what the editors wanted was an "off the top of your head" reaction to topics ranging from financial record keeping, consolidated schools, funeral customs or 4-H leadership to family fun. Sometimes they sought a regional attitude and we would invite other farm couples in for dinner and discussion. Once we tested adult games and party refreshments in the same evening.

Many of the feature articles in the Family Living section of *Farm Journal* were staff written from the opinions sent in by test-group members. When we were quoted, we were paid—$3 for a sentence, $10 for a paragraph. My living room couch, purchased from a second-hand barn, was rebuilt and upholstered with those small checks. Sometimes I can picture the series of clippings which restored it:

How to use broccoli stems, peeled and sliced, in Chinese dishes. Avoiding hardening of the attitudes in setting priorities. Tackling life as an adventure instead of an endurance test. Holding onto happy moments while heading for the next hump.

When *Farm Journal* decided to publish its first cookbook, we were asked for suggestions on organization. In responding to that, I confessed that I read cookbooks the way some people take to mysteries, even to ghoulishly wondering, upon reading obituaries, "What will happen to her cookbooks?"

Before beginning this column, I talked with several people in the writing field and they brushed aside my negative thoughts. "Of course you can do it," one stated firmly. "Just list your topics, run them through your philosophy, and you've got it made."

I basked in the confidence they expressed but backed away from trying to pinpoint my philosophy. Six months later when an old friend, who has had years of editorial experience, said he liked the philosophy expressed in my column, I asked him to tell me what he read.

"Three things," he told me. "You feel that for you living in the country offers more options for a better life. Your wonder and awe at the interrelationships of all the living things upon your acres show your belief in a force or power beyond mere humans. And, do you realize how often you write about living in the NOW? You can't change yesterday. You may not be around tomorrow. But this moment, this hour is happening."

Probably too many years of writing up bits of educational philosophy negated my responses even to the word. "Philosophy" brings to mind hours of word shiftings and typing up noble sounding paragraphs to go into some drawer or closet. I couldn't name two people today who could tell me any philosophy so laboriously concocted.

However, I did write down the three points my editorial friend had read in the "Orange Mailbox" and I've kept them on my desk. When readers write, I check their comments against those ideas. A college professor in British Columbia and a librarian in New Jersey responded to the positive force of humor in a classroom and both suggested laughter as a prescription for daily living. Hooting and howling uproariously seem easier in the country.

My world has widened and the list of topics I want to learn more about has grown each week. Last summer when I started to find the names of the weeds on my acres, I had difficulty finding reference materials. Through readers and other gardening writers I've acquired a whole shelf of books. Since I wrote about the taste treat of spring parsnips, my mailbox has received copies of six articles on this hearty vegetable. A Burpee horticulturalist sent me a copy of their ad for broccoli in the 1886 catalog. I never knew there was such a vegetable until 1942.

There are stories behind every familiar object on this farm and life in more shapes and forms than I'll ever learn in a lifetime—even with the help which comes through my mailbox.

NOTHING IS HIDDEN in March. The landscape has a naked, vulnerable, unprotected look. Encroaching bushes stagger along the edges of the lawn and fields, and wind-piled litter from passing cars sits muddied and nasty along the roadside. The farm colors are austere shades of gray and brown and black, with just the promise of some lift and life in the swelling of the willow branches and the rose-brown maple buds. The promise of spring and a new beginning.

Over the years, during this pre-spring drabness, I have wondered what the promise was which brought the first family here to clear the land that is now mine. Looking out across my acres and wandering through the rooms of this 170-year-old house, I have tried to project myself backwards in time to feel what it must have been like living in the first house on this hill.

Like most of my projections, forward or backward, the images proved to be pure fiction. I pictured a lonely woman, uprooted from a settled community near the Massachusetts border (as it is today), gazing with fear at the impenetrable forest surrounding her home, being literally prepared to keep the wolf from the door.

The truth, the facts I found in studying the history of Union and the surrounding area, seems even stranger than fiction.

Reuben Hills left Hawke (now Danville), New Hampshire about 1803 and bought land along the east side of the St. Georges River from the village of Union up through Appleton and Hope. It seems reasonable to assume that he must have been a successful man in New Hampshire in order to have money enough to purchase so many acres in Maine.

Hills built a saw mill at the foot of Sennebec Pond and since this town, only about thirty years old, had 600 residents when he arrived, there was a need for planks and boards. Within ten years the population of Union doubled.

What seems strange to me, what keeps tossing up questions, and stirring my curiosity and my imagination, is the fact that Reuben Hills was sixty-one years old when he did this. That was well past the prime of life according to life expectancy of that century. Futhermore, he was the father of twelve children (two of those had died young) and a grandfather. And when Reuben Hills set forth, like the patriarchs of the Bible, he led his family, and their families, into the wilderness.

I speculate like a true mystery fan. What might have happened back there in New Hampshire at the beginning of the 19th century which could account for the uprooting of so many families? And why—out of all the known lands opening up in this new country—did they pack up and move to Union? All of them?

The records indicate that Reuben was not an open-handed patriarch. His seems to have been a philosophy of "work and win." He deeded land to his sons, his sons-in-law and his nephews with specific terms of payment. He employed them at his mill, paid them for timber from their acres, arranged terms for lumber for their houses and barns—but it was business all the way.

Reuben Hills was obviously a careful and capable business man. When nature dealt old Reuben a mighty blow one spring by sending such a freshet that the whole course of the river moved from the east side of the valley beside Hills' mill to flow along the ledges on the west, he turned it to his advantage. He built two log dams, thus forming a mill pond twice the size of the old one, and this afforded him water power for more than one mill.

The lonely lady I envisioned in my old house had actually arrived here surrounded by relatives and, with their aid, was soon living in the original house, which had two fair-sized rooms and three tiny ones. Scars exposed in remodeling indicate that there were two fireplaces set on a brick arch. Old Reuben used the valley clay for local brick baking.

The morning sun warmed her kitchen as it does mine, but the sight of the pond, the glorious view I enjoy, was shut off to her. Doors to the three small rooms sealed out the sweep of the north wind, but those partitions have since been removed.

I knew that the addition to this house had been made before 1830, but only recently could I guess why it was done then. I found a head count of Union school districts done in 1826 which showed that Reuben and his family totaled sixty-one. Nine of them were in my house. Surely that was the right time to add five rooms.

When I took down the molding in what is my guest room, one section was labeled "over the organ," so that room with its narrow fireplace must have been the parlor.

The day the New Jersey van unloaded here they brought my furniture in through the wide double doors on the west. I recall remarking that it looked as though the doors had been built big enough to accommodate a coffin. I now know that it was only a few years before those doors were built that the Union selectmen authorized money for the first hearse.

Fiction and facts. This in-between season, when melting snow and mud and puddles hamper outdoor chores always sends my mind skittering. And I wonder about the first woman who lived in my house. What did she think about in March? Did this new home fulfill the promise which brought her here? And although of course it's none of my business, what do you suppose happened down in New Hampshire around 1800 to instigate the exodus of all those Hills families?

LATE ONE EVENING the father of a student phoned to ask if I had really told his son that he had chains in his head. Chains? It took a few moments to think back over the school day and find some link between the telephone question and the multiple interactions which had occurred during seven class periods.

The room was dark Outside the stars were bright in the clear night sky and the words, "You haven't seen stars until you've seen the night sky in Shiraz" unexpectedly came into my mind. And with those words a flash of memory of an August night in our blueberry field when, in explaining our compass directions to a young man from Iran, I found that my perception of the heavens hung on a demonstration my fifth grade teacher had done long years past in a darkened classroom.

And then I remembered the school day activity which had prompted that father's phone call and question. Yes, we had talked about chains. I had even drawn a great log chain across the chalk board as an illustration. The impromptu lecture started from the usual "Why do we have to study this *stuff?*" followed by a flood of negative complaints about school in general.

I had responded by explaining that learning is not a matter of sticking isolated bits of knowledge into one's head at random. In order to lock in so that they can be used, facts, methods, or ideas must be linked to something which is already there. Obviously one can't learn long division without having first acquired the ability to add, subtract and multiply. A student who collects beer labels as a hobby is more apt to remember that Milwaukee is in Wisconsin and that lager doesn't mean a man with a chain saw.

Yes, I had told his son that he had chains in his head—imaginary links of knowledge—forged at home, in school and at play since the day of his birth. And that everything he learned made it possible to learn more.

The parent accepted my explanation and I stepped outside to look up at the night sky and let my mind wander over the many links added to my chain of knowledge because one summer an exchange student from Iran lived here on the farm. His home was in Shiraz, high above sea level, where the atmosphere, dry and free of smog, made more stars visible.

Sampson, our Iranian guest, told us legends of Persepolis and showed us pictures of the animals—including a unicorn—in the sculptured friezes on the ruins of the great double stairways.

I never step upon a Persian carpet without remembering his demonstration of how each strand was tied in, or his imitation of the chanting of the weavers as they vocalized the pattern design—a much more complicated version of "knit one, purl one" with rows of women knotting the rich colors of the wool.

Krishna, who came the next year, couldn't speak English when he left his home in Nepal and he had only a few weeks of orientation in India and the days on shipboard before he reached this farm. The children undertook his education. Perhaps recalling their infant days, they led him through the house and around the fields naming what they passed and expecting him to repeat the words.

He puzzled over "sand" on the beach and the "sandwiches" we ate picnicking there. I explained that the bread-enclosed nourishment was named for the Earl of Sandwich who instructed his servant to place meat between slices of bread so the Earl wouldn't have to leave the gambling tables to appease his hunger. I could only guess how that noble family received its name. Perhaps "wich" was a corruption or misspelling of "wick" which meant town or hamlet and the first Sandwich folks lived beside a sandy shore.

By the time Krishna left for a stay in Arkansas two months later, he had had a crash course in English—speaking, reading, and writing—and his first message told us he had had to "bye a new suet case."

From Sampson and Krishna, and later from our student guests from India, many new chains of knowledge were started. When the reeds stir beside the swimming area I recall Krishna's fear of crocodiles and the tales he told of predators in his country. When I read news reports from the Middle East I think of Sampson's difficulties living as a Christian in an Islamic culture and on cloudless nights I remember his descriptions of the stars above Shiraz.

And then I remember the magic in that long-ago classroom when the teacher poked holes in a cardboard box to let light from an extension cord come through. But first she started with the Big Dipper and the North Star so we had a familiar link on which to hook new learning.

The day I told my students that they had chains in their heads I was trying to communicate the idea that by keeping the mind active, learning is easier—it can become exciting. I wanted them to understand that all experiences and the feelings which accompany them are stored within the mind, waiting like dormant magnets. And they can be temporarily withdrawn from one's memory bank, polished up, and used.

When something heard or seen or read sets off that feeling of deja vu or just a niggling sense of something familiar, learning to pause and wait helps bring forth treasures from this memory bank. Haven't you found yourself saying something and then suddenly exclaiming, "I didn't know I knew that!"

SATURDAY MORNING the usual half-dozen blue jays raced each other from the hemlock windbreak to the compost pile and then rested in the pear tree loudly discussing their findings. The two groups of chickadees came to the feeder by the dining room window. Members of Group One approached cautiously with a reconnoitering pause on the garage roof to check the safety of the situation while Group Two birds zoomed straight in from the south. The aerial ballets when their approaches coincided were feats to admire.

Later that day I sorted out the winter vegetables, cooked the last of the leeks and some winter squash, and hauled several pails of seeds and peelings to the garden just at dusk.

Sunday morning the tempo of the blue jay noises brought me to the kitchen window to find dozens of the brilliant creatures arguing over the compost scraps. Small Red, the lone squirrel, feasted calmly on the back lawn but kept a watchful eye on the jay congregation. Within ten minutes (alerted by the jays' loud chorus?) the pear tree was suddenly in bloom with yellow birds. Before I could get the field glasses to see whether they were goldfinches or evening grosbeaks, they lifted off, circled briefly to buzz the asparagus bed and disappeared.

As I watched them swoop out of sight—wishing I knew enough about flight patterns to aid in identification—a downy woodpecker flew in to investigate the pear tree and a sea gull landed beside the orange pile of peelings.

After complaining most of the winter because birds ignored my offerings of seeds, cleaning the cellar and refrigerator triggered a spectacular change in the aerial activity over my acres. This compost collection of greens and squash pulp was spread before the winged population while they were dealing with the many changes the lengthening daylight and melting snows were already making in their survival patterns.

Changes—however small—cause other changes. In spring

the renewal of life after the winter rest presents so many changes that there seems to be a rhythmic stirring in the very ground beneath my feet. The eye of the pond—where the river flows in—is widening each day and the color of the ice cover is becoming gray and dull. The frost heaves a fresh collection of rocks to the surface and the draining hillsides help fill the low meadow where the frogs will soon be serenading the season as they fill the waters with eggs for this year's pollywogs.

Why is it then since life is change—seed to maturity, dawn to dusk, winter into spring—that human beings seem so often to fear and resist change?

Such resistance is usually easier to see in others. When a proposal for some community innovation is suggested the immediate response is "But we have always . . ." A friend complains about the long dreary winters but resists the idea of going south for a month because it's too different. Rather like feeling more comfortable with the familiar uncomfortableness.

Sometimes I feel like a four-pound lobster in a three-pound shell—cramped, smothered, limited. Probably the lobster doesn't waste much time pondering whether he should or shouldn't go for the big change. When his body feels too uncomfortable, he crawls under a rock or reef, scratches his hard shell loose, and stretches out in his tender pink membrane. Vulnerable, yes. The tides can toss him against a rock. Larger fish can attack his unprotected form. But only by opening himself up to this risk can the lobster grow.

Human beings don't have to shed their old shells all at once and become totally vulnerable. But just chipping away at self-imposed restrictions involves risk.

Somewhere I read a parody of an old proverb which might make a good springtime motto—"Fools rush in where angels fear to flutter and thus get places angels don't—and have a better time." Fools according to whose definition?

It may be my age or metabolism or the quickening and stirring of the plants and birds down through this valley but I'd like to haul half the stuff in this farmhouse out into the backyard and have a huge symbolic bonfire and dance around it.

Why don't I? Old habits persist—as confining as a too tight lobster shell. Financial fears hang on like heavy fog and procrastination prevails in spite of my seasonal discontent. But the seeds of change are sprouting. Pitching out the remains of last year's garden crops brought birds and beauty to my backyard and an early leaven of my spirit.

Neither plants nor people can grow without changes and spring seems the time to loosen the tenacity of old habits. And to remember Emily Dickinson's "A little Madness in the Spring is wholesome even for the King."

M Y W O R L D is wet and windy. The flooded east field looks like a farm pond where gusts roil the surface as though schools of fish were feeding there.

The last drifts of snow are melting in the garden and I'm eyeing the parsnip patch with anticipation. The winter's cold will have turned the starch to sugar. They'll be fresh and firm—a spring taste treat.

The mere mention of "parsnip" brings a dreamy look into the eyes of vegetable connoisseurs—those who know the flavor of freshly dug, well-wintered roots—or those with nostalgic memories of parsnip stew. Yet this carrot-shaped food elicits strong negative noises from others and is sometimes rated among the most disliked vegetables. This may be because these folks tried parsnips in September before they attained full flavor or have only known store produce so long removed from the soil that both the sweetness and tender texture had deteriorated.

Many home gardeners never bother to plant parsnips because they are a long season crop. In Maine they are usually planted in early May and harvested the next April. Neat types, who like to clean their gardens in the fall and leave them tidy and naked through the winter, find rows of crops disorderly. Parsnip fanciers usually dig and enjoy some in November, cover some with a heavy mulch of leaves so they can be pried out in December, and leave the rest stored—gaining flavor—for spring and the thawing ground.

Back in ancient Rome the Emperor Tiberius was so fond of parsnips that he had them imported each year from Germany. From the Rhine valley they were imported to England and brought to America with the first colonists in Virginia. The American Indians liked the sweet nut-like flavor and passed along the cultivation of these roots from tribe to tribe.

Early American cookbooks included recipes for both parsnip stew and soup. For the stew salt pork was fried crisp and cubed. Onions were sautéd in the pork fat, potatoes and parsnips added with just enough water to cook. When these were tender, "good milk with cream" was added, heated gently and then the cubed pork was stirred in. Soup was made with lamb or beef but venison could be used. Cut into bite-sized pieces, the meat was simmered with three cups of "soft spring water" per pound until "breaking into shreds." Large parsnips were chopped, fried in butter, and then added to the meat about fifteen minutes before serving.

French fried parsnips are elegant but most people prefer to pan fry parboiled roots in butter. Because of the sugar content of these roots, care must be taken that they don't scorch. Some country cooks mash parsnips and potatoes together while others alternate layers of sliced parsnips and potatoes dotted with butter and bake them with cream or cream and milk. Definitely not low-calorie but delicious.

It is necessary to have well-worked soil for growing parsnips and the addition of some sand, compost, and wood ashes will promote longer, smoother roots. English garden books recommend double digging to a depth of two feet since most good parsnips grow at least twelve inches long. The loose loam prevents forked roots.

Since parsnip seeds lose their vitality if kept more than a year, it is important to use fresh seed. I prefer to plant in a row about the width of the rake—zig-zagging the seeds so those down the center (hopefully) won't be too close to those on the outsides. I scatter a few radish seeds in with them because these rapid germinaters help to break up the soil crust as they grow. Parsnips are slow to germinate—sometimes more than twenty-one days.

The seeds need to be firmly in contact with the grains of the soil in order to root. Country gardeners have their individual ways of tamping after the seeds have been covered. One farmer firmly maintains that you can't get a fine stand of parsnips unless you tromp on them—tromp them down good. He says he learned this the year his cows got loose and crossed the patch he'd just planted to parsnips. Every seed grew. Best parsnip crop he ever had.

I've tried walking a board atop the row, tamping with a hoe, and walking back and forth over the row. The walking patch did best, but I think I'll try this a few more years before recommending it.

The seedlings need to be thinned so each has about a four-inch circle to grow in, and they must be weeded until the green tops shade the soil. Then just do the general weed hoeing while they grow for the 120 days it takes to produce that special, sweet, parsnip flavor.

In England they serve steamed parsnips, cold, with celery and mayonnaise and call it poor man's lobster salad. This may be the week to try it.

IN THE SPRING a woodchuck's fancy turns to mating and then eating—in that order. Have you ever given much thought to the love life or lust life of woodchucks? There's the male chuck. It's spring. He has slept in his fur coat all winter in an unventilated chamber. Certainly hasn't brushed his teeth. Six months of hibernation have used up his autumn fat so his skin is loose and flabby. Not attractive nor appealing. Tatty looking.

Yet in this lubbery, musky, musty condition, what does this rough-furred creature do as soon as he crawls out of his winter bed? Before he finds himself a full meal? He sets off waddling through mud and melting snows in search of a female. Sniffing over the soggy fields, aggressively bloodying any males who get in his way, the woodchuck at this season is adamant and pugnacious.

Judging by the increase in woodchuck population each spring, female chucks must also awaken with activated libido because they accept the attentions of these disheveled, den-musky males. Come May Day, most female woodchucks' burrows harbor two to eight tiny hairless chucklings. And if the foxes don't feast on them, they'll grow quickly into voracious vegetarians—garden thieves.

People who grew up with Mother West Wind stories, where Johnny Chuck is a friendly, pudgy character, usually react strongly when they discover their gardens decimated overnight by these insatiable nibblers. Injuries to man and livestock can result from stepping into woodchucks' burrows. Tractors can break through and tip, and mower teeth can be blunted and broken by the rocks and rough piles of dirt tossed up by the woodchucks in their burrow-building.

War on woodchucks is a country ritual. Many farmers have a vantage point from which they aim their guns at the garden thieves. An upper story window of house or barn provides a good view before the grasses grow to hide the raw earth piles which locate the den entrance.

But the woodchucks always build in another exit—sometimes several extras. While woodchucks appear pudgy and dull, the slightest sound or movement will alert their senses and send them scuttling with great speed into their holes. Almost immediately curiosity prompts them to peer forth, but because their ears and eyes are so close to the tops of their heads, they manage to peek and duck and avoid attack.

Young woodchucks, playing like puppies, are a delight to watch—or would be if one could forget that each will grow into a bean-muncher and broccoli-eater. Adult chucks, sprawled on top of their dirt piles, basking in the sunshine with a belly full of vegetables, look as friendly as a nice old dog. When they sit up on their haunches, nibbling on food held in their front paws, alert and bright-eyed, they have a certain charm. Unless it's your garden cucumbers they're chewing.

Country folks have tales to tell of individual methods of eliminating woodchucks from the land. One grandfather claims he hasn't had a chuck near his garden since he buried a two-weeks' accumulation of used Pampers in his woodchuck holes. Another landowner swears by his method—shoveling dog droppings down into each burrow he finds.

My dog, Miss Badger, gets her exercise and recreation searching out and destroying woodchucks from spring until fall. She used to deposit them on the front steps and await praise but now, judging by her burps, I guess she devours them. My garden is free from this predator, but my dog carries a musty groundhog odor all summer long.

Can nothing good be said about this overgrown member of the squirrel family? Regarded as soil movers and aerators, they do—like giant earthworms—mix earth, permit water and air to enter and improve drainage. It has been estimated that one woodchuck moves 400 pounds of earth in his burrow building. Thus, if you have ten woodchucks (and they do like their privacy), those creatures would move two tons of earth for you. Maybe not where you want it moved, but it might be to your advantage.

Skunks, foxes and snakes move into deserted burrows, and since these do destroy mice and insects, this might be a chuck's gift of value. If only they weren't such constant eaters and if they could be persuaded to dine on something besides my kitchen garden, I might not mind woodchucks sharing my land—after a good spring airing out.

MARCH CAN BE an irritating month. The weather is fickle. Just as the sun gets high enough to warm the world and melt the banks of snow, another storm dumps a fresh supply. What *did* melt freezes, and the driveway becomes a skidway. When I try to back the car north into the garage, it slides east into the woodpile.

The pond which pleasured me in December as a glorious expanse of pure white, I now see as a monotonous dull cover imprisoning the water. I'm impatient for the opening—the moving water reflecting the colors of the sky and, at night, twinkling back the lights along the valley. I'm disenchanted by the wind sculptured drifts across my garden and the piles of snow I paid to have plowed from the driveway.

Although winter lingers, some March mornings are so clean and fresh that when I watch the dawn the word *renewal* seems to sing and echo in my head. The amber willow branches are warming into gold. The swelling buds of the swamp maples lend a rosy glow to the lowlands along the cove while the crowns of the white birches defy a color description— they just vibrate with life.

A small red squirrel arrived this week to feed upon the seeds the birds scatter from the feeder. Unlike the gray squirrel, who speeds out of sight if there's the slightest movement at the window, Small Red looks me straight in the eye and goes on nibbling. His coat is so thick and glossy that wherever he has been during the winter months, his diet must have been ample.

Watching this small creature scampering across the snow with his striped tail spread for balance, I was reminded of my high school days. Wearing a red squirrel's tail was important. First, of course, the striped furry object must be presented to you by the young man who had shot the squirrel thus proclaiming his skill in marksmanship and his interest in the manly art of hunting and using guns. Second, and most important, if you had a red squirrel's tail pinned to your school sweater, everyone could see that you had an admirer.

I wonder now if there wasn't an offensive odor in those crowded classrooms as more and more females pinned freshly cut squirrel tails upon their budding bosoms. And what kind of remarks were made in the teachers' room as the faculty discussed that status symbol, knowing (as teachers do), "This too shall pass."

Most general nature books state that the red squirrel is not a desirable resident because it feeds upon the eggs and the young fledglings from birds' nests. Small Red must have a family somewhere in my woods but so far he comes alone to feed and to watch me watching him.

March seems to stir a gastronomical unrest—an indefinite craving for something different at mealtimes. The snow and frost still seal in the parsnips and salsify, and the last green leaves of kale are too scant to gather. Several seed catalogs are offering new varieties of hot peppers and just reading these turns my thoughts to Mexican meals.

Some years ago a foods editor for a family magazine did a series on the "spice of the month," and she wrote that mustard belongs to March. Perhaps hot mustard? A friend who earned his way through college working in Chinese restaurants taught me to make a hot mustard which will raise the hairs upon your forehead and bring tears of appreciation. Three tablespoons of dry mustard plus one scant teaspoon of sugar blended to a creamy consistency with vinegar makes truly hot mustard. Those preferring milder but still pungent mustard might blend some of the hot with the usual store jar variety.

Craig Claiborne in his *New York Times* food writings said that mustard symbolizes indifference. That Chinese hot mustard will erase indifference unless used with discretion.

Waiting for spring weather, waiting for the mud and frost to go away can be irritating. Innovations in cooking and trying new lighting methods on seedlings help survival in this month but as the day-light hours lengthen, being outside becomes a primary urge.

March is also maple syrup time, and I note with some sadness that the long row of sugar maples below the farmhouse is slowly declining. They've been tapped by many different residents upon this hill and show the scars. The tales of drinking sap to aid the growth of unborn babies, to clear the head of winter cobwebs, and to stir the libido are not just told in Maine.

Standing on a snowbank watching the chickadees trying to drink the sap leaking from twigs, drinking the cold mildly sweet sap myself, and sniffing the fresh breezes, does stir new life.

It's time to force-bloom some forsythia, seek out some pussy willows for contrast, and, depending upon the fickle wind and weather, hike down to watch the skunk cabbage melt the ice around itself and proclaim the coming of spring.

APRIL

"MARCH" SOUNDS HARSH and has connotations of weariness and dreary journeys with cold and tired feet. But "April" has a lilt to it. I find myself alternating between impulses to sail bits of bark as boats down the run-off streams (betting on their safe sailing through the culvert) and the need to stand in silent wonder at the vast tilting and revolving of this ponderous planet which has brought the sunset back again to my kitchen window.

In January it was necessary to walk through the house to the guest room to watch the setting sun. On June twenty-first two tall spruce trees on top of the ridge will frame the sun as it sets directly across from the corner windows above my orange sink. The morning sun no longer creeps up over the tall pines but, having moved northward, springs up beyond the orchard as though it couldn't wait to warm the world.

There's an excitement about beginnings and April is another beginning in the spiral of my country years, an onward, upward continuity of living and participating in the cycle of growth and harvest. The annual miracle of spring with the stirrings of the soil and the quickenings of the plants is proof that life persists despite earthquakes, volcanic eruptions, and human follies. This miracle is also a powerful, pulsing reminder that I do not control the life on my acres.

Living in the country tends to focus my thinking towards a fairly small world but one I know well and see as a whole. I've learned what influences good production on my farm and have adjusted to what can be changed and what must be accepted. Garden records show an average of 112 frost-free nights. Not necessarily warm, growth-promoting nights—just those without white frost. If the seed catalog says 110 days to maturity, I know about what my chances of success will be.

The day the ice goes out of the pond I start my tomato seeds. If tomato seedlings stay in the house too long they tend to get spindly. If they're set out before the soil is warm, they just sit and sulk. Ice-out time makes a reasonable, easy-to-remember time to start the seeds and gives me the feeling of working with nature.

Until I moved to this house on the hill overlooking the pond, I had never seen any body of water free itself from its strait jacket of ice. The first year I described the pond in December as ". . . all pure and white. It stretches north for two miles giving the valley a tranquil, restful look." In March I saw the same scene as " . . . so dull and monotonous. The whole valley appears dead and boring and I long for open, splashing, reflecting water."

We used to place bets on the day the pond would be free of ice and the winner could choose dessert. Ice-out brought chocolate roll with whipped cream, lemon pie, blueberry steamed pudding, Indian pudding, and others now forgotten. Then the ice-out picnic and watching for the first sign of the loons—all part of the excitement of April.

The house used to be full of flats and pots and cans of seedlings until the time required to water and turn and re-transplant the hundreds of green growing things brought more frustration than pleasure. I do start eggplant and peppers because there are certain varieties I want to test. But I tend only enough seedlings for my garden plan. There may be some status in having the earliest broccoli in the neighborhood but rather than tend seedlings indoors I'll use my time to be outside sniffing the world now that April's here.

The earth, giving up its winter rigidity, exudes many different fragrances: the gentle pungent scent of wet oak leaves, the sharp, sweet odor of the first green grasses, the soft, rich aroma of the dark compost.

The soil is for growing and life is for living. Spring reminds me of the constant changes within the framework of eternal continuity. Only by cooperating with the soil and understanding the laws of nature can I garden with pleasure. I need to grow my food. I need to continue the gardening experiments for my writing assignments. April, the month of renewal, reminds me that my acres must be managed to provide me with time to celebrate being and feeling alive, time to slow down and savor my joy in living here. Joy is the best harvest.

THERE'S A TALE about an art gallery where one particular abstract painting didn't seem to attract any buyers. One day someone rehung it upside down and doubled the price. Within a week an interested customer paid the price and cheerfully carried it off.

That story may or may not be true but the principles it illustrates are worth remembering. Simple solutions often work and turning things or problems upside down or round about stimulates the need to view them with a fresh perspective.

Browsing through some gardening books including *Burrage On Vegetables*, I noted that in his basic vegetable garden plan Albert Burrage had divided his space with a center path running east to west. To simplify rotation, each year he reverses the crops grown on the south side with those planted in the north-side soil. No long detailed advice on setting in broccoli where the beets had been nor even the traditional (and sound) admonition to exchange root crop spaces with above ground producers.

This probably caught my eye because Burrage's garden division is the opposite of mine. My center path runs north and south. Considering my space divided his way—a total reversal—immediately stimulated ideas of new planting blocks.

In spite of tidy graph paper plans and photo records, I often end up planting some vegetables in the same spot where they grew the year before. My excuses are the confusion caused by the hordes of healthy black flies which insist upon joining me and the enthusiam which multiplies with each hour in the sun and soil.

Rotating crops helps prevent disease spores from accumulating and discourages the pests which tend to move in where they find a favorite food supply. Because plants are selective and take what they need from the soil, rotating insures that one kind of vegetable isn't depleting your loam.

The history of agriculture in this country is full of records of waste and abuse. The promise of plenty—lands stretching westward waiting for the plow—resulted in the most rapid rate of wasteful land use in the history of the world. By growing the same crops on the same fields, the early American farmers wore out land it had taken thousands of years to build. Erosion carried the misused topsoil off into rivers, and the families moved west repeating the abuse and destruction across the continent.

Early explorers along our east coast sailed up the rivers and wrote about the clear waters. But before our Declaration of Independence was signed in 1776, most of those rivers flowed black with mud as they washed the fertile layers of earth down to the sea.

Rotating small beds of carrots and beans and feeding the soil in a backyard garden may seem like a minute contribution toward preserving the thin skin of this planet which supports all life. The results of soil care, however, seem to be contagious.

A friend, who always has a few cattle in his barn, claims that his garden gulps down the piles he hauls there from each stable clean out. "One day it's there and then it's gone. The land just eats it. Must be needy."

I can only estimate the numbers of bales of hay I've used on my rhubarb bed since I first transplanted one pale green plant over there more than thirty years ago. Certainly in the neighborhood of 300 bales plus truckloads of old newspapers and magazines. The heavy clay soil in that east field used to dry and crack in July. Walking on it was like treading across a paved parking lot.

The earth has taken in the hay and newsprint and all other additions of manure and leaves and sawdust. It now has a springy feeling when walked upon and a velvety texture when sifted through the hands.

I do believe the old line "If weeds grow in it, that soil will grow vegetables." But quality, flavored produce? If weeds will grow, chop them up and feed them back to that earth. Dump in the potato peels and limp lettuce leaves. Stir in your coffee grounds and a bag of dirt from beside the brook where you fish. Feed the little organisms and then plant and let your soil feed you. Using all organic matter you find available to nourish the garden is a simple solution which does work.

Reversing my garden path will give a new look to the whole area. It may confuse the cutworms. The grandchildren and the dog—accustomed to past routes—may trample a bit at first but the turn-about concept has taken hold. Now if the cold winds will just ease off for a few hours.

L I N E 1 3—Capital gain distributions. Back to the book of instructions. But this skips from what to do on line 6 to how to use line 17. Try the paperback *The Complete List of IRS Deductions*. No index. Flip through to information for doing Schedule D. No mention of capital gain distributions.

It is now 2 a.m. I know the dictionary won't help and it's not the hour to phone anyone. Try another book, *Take It Off*, which is set up alphabetically. There's a bit on capital improvements and capital losses—no mention of distributions. This "easy reference" for filling out tax forms has information on contraceptives, examples of what to do if you're a wholesale liquor dealer purchasing shares of stock in a distillery, and a reported case of an octogenarian who was allowed to deduct expenses for an office in his home used for handling his own investments. Was he making capital gain distributions?

Do you ever wonder about the personalities of the people who write the small print for the income tax instructions? Those paragraphs of explanations full of "unless" and "only if" which invariably conclude with "For additional information send for Publication No. . . . ." Sometimes I picture these rule writers arriving home after a long day at the IRS office saying, "Whew—what a job! But I finally made it complicated enough to frustrate folks from Penobscot Bay to Puget Sound."

Or I visualize these instruction constructors standing before the final judgement gates justifying their earthly existence according to supplement number, page, and line. And I like to think that St. Peter or his current aide would gaze in amazement at the righteousness of those—created in His image who have caused so many hours of frustration to so many form-filling human beings.

There is one positive element in working through the task of filing income taxes by the long form. It forces me to take a look at just what I did do with my income and—while the ice-out signals the beginning of another year of growing and changing—consider better ways of managing money.

However, that opportunity for self-improvement does not alleviate the resentment of the hours entailed in messing around with figures. If I set an arbitrary pay scale of $10 per hour to wade through all the schedules, I end up being excessively annoyed by what I consider waste because in less than half a second the government can spend this and more for some senator to enjoy an elegant lunch in Paris or Peking.

Perhaps I approach the whole process with a negative attitude. My feelings about filling out nine forms so I can pay the government the money I'd like to spend for several loads of manure and lime might be more cheerful if I would read the instruction pamphlets as interesting social science. Certainly there's much to be learned about life in these United States which I just don't come across in my country living.

Take vacations and vasectomies. A family doctor might suggest considering these in reverse order but the IRS tries to be alphabetical. Travel expenses should be reasonable and necessary. When families and couples can't agree on where to vacation, it's comforting to read that the income tax people have been making decisions about such travel deductions for years. I like the words "expenditures appropriate to the development and pursuit of a trade or business." Pursue and deduct. Develop in Dublin. Be reasonable in Rio.

Relax and read on: "You are an officer of a domestic corporation with assets of more than $1 million—" I can't even imagine $1 million—"You can deduct the cost of repairs—that do not add to the value or increase the life of the property." Why would anyone contract to have repairs done if these would not increase the life of the property? Out there in the IRS world there are American citizens living quite different life-styles from my days here on the farm.

The friendly message from the Commissioner of Internal Revenue tells me that there are many people wanting to make voluntary contributions to reduce the public debt. At the moment that sounds just about as sensible as carrying a teacup full of water to put out a grass fire in a twenty-acre field.

So I'm still feeling negative. But the tax forms must be filled out and I'd better accept what I can not change. At least I won't have to suffer through this again for another year. Except the state forms need to be completed too . . .

IN A MAGAZINE ARTICLE on personal time management I once read one writer's opinion that seventy minutes per day was sufficient for housekeeping tasks. I assume this author meant in homes where there are no two-year-olds and where other children have been taught that they are not guests but must share in the repetitive pickup and clean-up.

Now seventy minutes per day adds up to 490 minutes per week or eight hours plus ten minutes. This might be interpreted as doing all the chores in what would equal one day at the office and thus having all the rest of the before and after work hours blissfully free. But just how do meals and dishes fit in?

However, the idea of an upward limit for time expended on necessary maintenance seemed positive, worth considering. A house with two adults zipping about on cleaning chores for seventy minutes each day would be twice as tidy as the home of a single adult. Wouldn't it? Or did that author imply that with double occupancy each individual should then only have to spend thirty-five minutes per day vibrating to the rhythm of a vacuum cleaner, folding laundry, and sorting out the junk mail?

It seems obvious that a four room house would get a better clean-up than an eight room house. Yet it doesn't quite follow that eight mess-creating adults in a four room house would be more likely to end up with a spotless environment than four folks with eight rooms—still, of course, keeping the limit of seventy minutes per day for all necessary duties.

That article was trying to remind readers that everyone has twenty-four hours per day but most people could make better choices for their personal uses of this time if they would consider their priorities and alternatives. I reacted to one particular sentence.

Some friends, both retired army officers, live in an enormous old house in New Hampshire which is an ideal setting for the antiques they have inherited or acquired. During the winter they give each room a thorough cleaning. Years of military inspections have developed habits of neatness and high standards of cleanliness. But they have set their personal priorities and when April comes they turn their attention to the out-of-doors. The house receives minimum maintenance while they remain firm on their personal schedule of enjoying country living.

The "turn everything upside down" system of spring cleaning has gone out of style. Remember those horror weeks when all furniture was moved to porch or lawn, rugs were beaten on sagging clotheslines, overstuffed chairs were whammed with something like a metal tennis racket, and wiped over with vinegar-soaked sponges? When the cracks in the baseboards were scoured even if it meant using cotton-wrapped hairpins? Then there was the laborious task of putting it all back together again while tempers told of aching backs.

The increased intensity of light and the longer hours of daylight in April seem to stimulate a healthy restlessness, a passion for reform and change. Venting stirring energies on spring cleaning in the garden seems preferable to moving and beating up on muscle-taxing furniture.

True—thirty bales of wet banking hay weigh more than any of my overstuffed chairs, but, using writer Eric Sloane's gentle art of sliding, they can be maneuvered without strain. And I can hear the wind soughing in the thick pines while I work.

The April sunshine is still chilled by brisk breezes but once I've turned over the first spadeful of garden soil and sniffed the familiar and provocative earthy fragrance, I find it difficult to pull myself back to any indoor chores even for seven minutes a day.

This week I can dig and readily pull out the long reaching roots of quack grass and weeds. But there's a relentless kind of assertion in the growing world and within a few weeks these roots will have anchored themselves tenaciously by sending out hundreds of strong root tendrils, to grip the earth. What I remove this month from the rhubarb, asparagus, and strawberries will save hours of time later on.

Suggesting a time limit for gardening—minimum or maximum—would be ridiculous. But when personal time management is being considered, this is a good season to remember the closed-in feelings of January, the relentless fact that we will have black flies and mosquitoes before long and that this day and this week will never be again.

THE IMPORTANT HARVESTS of this farm are the impressions given to children who have lived or visited here, the memories they carry from their times upon these acres.

Last fall, my two-year-old granddaughter, Sara Beth, called my attention to a daddy longlegs she discovered in my living room. Then she pointed out a mommy longlegs and a baby longlegs. However, she soon announced that there were too many to name and wanted to know why I had so many of these creatures in my house.

I didn't have an answer and not a reference book in this house provided any information on these eight-legged invaders. Last week, just before my grandchildren arrived to help me celebrate my birthday, Judy Hawes' book, My Daddy Longlegs, came in at the book store. No sooner had it been read than Sara Beth and Jacob, aged four, asked for an escort for a trip through the cellar.

Armed with a flashlight, a plastic glass and an old post card, the three of us descended into the dirt-floored, cobwebby basement, stalked and captured two active specimens.

Back at the dining room table, we shared the magnifying glass to count the joints and knees and observe the second pair of legs which the daddy longlegs uses for hearing and smelling. Turning the plastic "cage," we could see the lookout tower on the top of the body with an eye on each side. We still need more information, because the body shapes of our Sennebec Hill daddy longlegs are not like the illustrations in the book. And when we have more time, we'll build a daddy longlegs box so we can watch them eat and dance and use their amazing second legs.

Jacob lives in a four-year-old world, part real, part make-believe, where every path has signs "What if . . . ?" On my birthday morning we followed the spring run-off water down across the fields to the pond shore. Behind the kitchen garden where the small stream comes through the culvert, the water ran clear. But in the field, twigs and grasses had been pushed by previous run-offs into small dams holding the water in pools. With our sturdy sticks, we cleared the channels and watched chocolate swirls as the free stream surged forward. With his new waterproof boots, Jacob could wade and splash and watch mud settle on his black toes.

We meandered as the run-off did, back and forth following the contours of the land until we reached the lower field. Here we stopped to examine and pick at the matted mounds piled up by force of water when the big snows melted. Soggy white patches like a scattered box of tissues wet down to earth caught our eyes. All along the swamp edge of the field, we found flattened weeds whose slim mahogany pods (like small snap beans) had burst to spill masses of white, like the down of milkweeds. I stuffed samples into my pocket.

Between the lapping waters of the pond edge and the firm mound of matted reeds and twigs left by the high water, the ground was scoured clean, the dark soil unlittered by a single leaf or twig. "It's very quiet here," said Jacob. "This is kind of a secret place. Maybe dragons lived here once. Or a trillion years ago some dinosaurs." Then, looking back the way we had come along the shore, he shook his head. "No. Dinosaurs couldn't get between those trees. They're much too large. But if a giant shark once lived in your pond, he could swim over and see this place. What's that?"

"That" was the leaf-littered hollow between the barrier berm—built up by drifted-in plant parts—and the oak-bordered bank. Wider than grandma's garage, the acidy water full of tough-fibered oak leaves discourages growth and looks like quivering quagmire. We out-spooked each other with scary stories and beat back all the monsters with our magic swords.

Late that afternoon Max, my younger grandson, became excited by something he was seeing. Kneeling down to his ten-month-old toddling size and following his eyes, I saw the sample weeds from the pond edge—now dry—exploding into miniature seed-carrying parachutes. Just the air currents of passing people were sending the bits of fluff up into space above the desk. The seeds—shaped like the eye of an embroidery needle—clung to individual feathery bits determined to find a place to root and grow more dogbane. We had identified the damp weed stalks and matted silk but had not expected the aerial display.

Daddy longlegs, dams, dark pools, and dogbane. What will my grandchildren remember from this April visit? And what farm excursions will their parents' memories prompt them to suggest next time they come?

THE "GREENING" RAIN came before I finished raking my lawns. The winds which came with it whistled erratically over the chimney like spring-happy kids blowing across the tops of bottles. The frogs quieted their evening chorus but still sent forth a serenade from the flooded east field where they produce pollywogs each April.

There's a period of time between the melting snows and ice-out and the green-up when there's a sense of transition. Time to view the lawns and gardens—to look at the distant hills still wearing faded brown grasses—and prepare for another season of growth. When I find myself writing mental lists of what needs to be done, long discouraging lists which no one person could possibly work through, I shake myself out of the "should, must and ought to" pessimistic mood by recalling joys of past springtimes.

Looking down into Katy Cove where migrating ducks are now feeding, I can see my children coming up the hill— soaked and muddy, glowing with pride. They had salvaged a dock. Discovering it in the cove where it had drifted down from some upper pond camp, they had maneuvered it along the shore and into our swimming area. When I went down to look (somehow restraining my reactions to the condition of their shoes after time underwater), I shared their feeling of accomplishment. Framed of logs and floored with heavy planks, the dock was larger than our kitchen. Two small children had towed this around rocks and sand bars at least an eighth of a mile to home port.

Our first farm dog, Mrs. Kitzel, helped initiate another spring ritual. From her German shepherd and collie ancestry she had a nose for locating varmints, and when she detected enemies beneath something she couldn't move, she barked for assistance. We'd lift a log or board and Mrs. Kitzel would catch the quarry—usually mice—snap them into oblivion and proceed to the next obstacle.

Long after that dog was gone, the turning over of logs and

rocks continued to be a spring habit. I still do it. While the ground remained cold, we seldom found more than sow bugs which, for reasons known only to them, the children called "seaweed bugs." We looked up their habits, found they spent most of their energy burrowing into rotten wood, and left them to recycle fallen trees in the woodland. These small creatures are of the animal group Crustacea—as lobsters are—and they can be pests in a strawberry bed, but mostly they're seen under logs and stones.

Watching frogs' eggs develop into tadpoles is part of official springtime happenings. They're quiet "pets" but offer a glimpse into the miracles of growth and change. In a glass jar they make no noise or fuss, no odor. Sometimes it's like peering back in time to the beginnings of life on this planet. One year more than a dozen matured to tiny frogs and then, the night before we planned to set them free with full honors, flags and music on a parade to the pond, they escaped and vanished. Not a trace was ever found.

Wallowing in squishy mud and staging soggy battles has been a part of spring letting go. Something about casting off the winter jackets, the freedom of movement, seems to stimulate friendly aggression. Probably there are few feelings quite as satisfactory as throwing—with good aim—a handful of frogs' eggs into someone's face.

Looking back through past Aprils, I find it was the contagious wonder the children found in roaming these acres that helped me to sense the season. Their asking me to "Come out and *be* in the world" continues to echo.

When the days are foggy and windless, it's possible to call across the pond and hear a clear echo of at least the last word. Long ago we recited nursery rhymes, and when you shouted "Humpty Dumpty," a clear response of "Dumpty" echoed back. Pure magic. I shout different lines now and delight in the returned words. Someday someone along the pond may send an echo message to surprise me.

Already the mornings are light at 4:30 and the stillness is sprinkled with the first bird songs. The banking hay must be hauled off to the rhubarb bed. Now it's just rolled away to let the bulbs push forth. Sitting on a bale, cradling my first cup of coffee, I find the memories of other farm springs are the best antidote to the panic which can infect my spirit if I let myself project into all the tasks the naked landscape reveals.

Perhaps like Jody Baxter in *The Yearling*, I'm a bit "addled with April"—finding excuses to delay the farm chores.

T HE AMERICAN TOADS have added their flute-like trill to the evening chorus of the peepers and frogs. The high pitched notes of the peepers sometimes sound like sleigh bells—clear and steadily repeated—but with each bell jangling separately. Occasionally there seems to be a harmony of the voices of these tiny frogs as though one *Hyla crucifer* had gathered a group and said, "Now all together boys!"

But when the toads pour forth their spring mating songs, the swamp serenade gains the sustained musical trill—somewhat like a hum and a whistle together—which softens the chorus. Some toads trill for more than thirty seconds before drawing in more air and these singing sounds are more pleasant than the mating music of the tree frogs or true frogs.

The wood frog's spring calling is sometimes compared to the clamorous quacking of ducks—rather hurried and urgent but not particularly musical. For the rest of the year these beige and brown frogs are silent. They're the longest leapers and can execute a reverse turn during their leaps to land facing their predators. Their silence and their protective coloring, which blends with the forest floor, make them somewhat difficult to find until they make a leap across one's woodland walk.

The voices of the leopard frog and pickerel frog are lower in tone than those of the peepers or the gray tree-frogs. The leopard frog's mating song has a quality of a snore about it while the pickerel frog maintains a prolonged note.

Apparently the different frog songs in the ponds and marshes serve to prevent interbreeding. Although the spotted leopard frog and pickerel frog with square spots are often confused by human observers, when the males sound their spring mating calls, the females go for the song which stirs their built-in senses. The loud calls also help to establish territories so there's room to get on with the fertilizing of the thousands of eggs each female lays.

When we set out to identify all the frogs and toads on this farm, we used the term "bullfrog" to indicate the male of each different group. In pursuing and observing the green frog—the one most often seen in the swimming area—we discovered the real bullfrog who sat among the reeds making his deep "jug-a-rum" sounds as evening approached. Full-grown, a bullfrog is the largest of the New England frogs but a young bullfrog resembles the green frog except that its head is broader and it has no lateral skin folds.

The small frogs which go leaping through the grass on the back lawn are young leopard frogs. One of them locates himself under the hose faucet each summer and can be easily captured for temporary viewing when children are visiting. Often called the "meadow" frog, this bright and beautiful amphibian has a habit of wandering far from the ponds and marshes. When startled by people or dogs, it makes long, low leaps through the grass and sometimes, when there are numbers of them, the lawn or meadow seems to be exploding frogs.

The green frogs sit in the shallow water along the beach with just their eyes visible above the surface and quickly submerge and swim away when they see their territory being invaded. The tadpoles of green frogs and bullfrogs may take several years to reach the "frog" stage and careful watching by the pond will often result in seeing some of the huge tadpoles wriggling into the shallows to feed.

Frog watching and spring chorus listening are part of the cycle of the seasons. Toad watching is a daily addition to gardening. When the local toads have sung their songs in the rites of romance, many of them come into the kitchen garden and settle in to devour injurious insects. Since one large hungry toad can consume up to 10,000 such creatures in one season, it's well to offer some toad apartments and shallow dishes of water. Old clay plant pots—half-buried and hay covered—will provide protective shelters and so will tepees built of bark debris from the woodpile. Toads drink by sitting in water and they'll appreciate fresh rations daily.

In return the American toad will guard your garden—reaching out his sticky tongue to capture cutworms and beetles. And next spring he'll burst into song again with his melodious flute-like trill.

MAY

DAFFODILS are an ancient Chinese symbol of good fortune. Roman gladiators promoted their good fortune—their survival—by carrying narcissus bulbs with them because the slimy juices would glue together the gashes and wounds they suffered in their bloody fights to entertain gore-loving spectators. As part of the standard first-aid kit of Roman soldiers, these bulbs of spring blossoms were carried to England where they flourished and inspired poets.

Each spring I find I need to renew the basics about these bulbs. Narcissus is the name of the genus, which includes daffodils and jonquils. Thus all daffodils are narcissus but all narcissus are not daffodils. It sounds so simple but I don't remember from year to year. I do remember reading that Americans import more than thirty million daffodil bulbs each year from Holland and that it takes twenty years to grow bulbs from a newly developed variety so that it can be offered to the public.

"Drift of gold" is a phrase which comes to mind in viewing these May blossoms while driving through the country. In some places where the yellow trumpet flowers cluster among white birches, bright against the green grass, the combination seems so right I want to go home and copy the effect.

The "fling" method is recommended for gardeners desiring a naturalized look of daffodils among trees and on edges of lawns. Buy bags of bulbs, fling them out across the lawn beneath the trees, and then dig in to plant them right there.

This is a fall activity. But now, in May, while along each street and road one can view the results of what someone else has accomplished in springtime beauty, catalogs and special-offer folders of bulbs for autumn planting are arriving from mail-order firms. Some glowing daffodils lift their blooms eighteen inches above the ground while others nestle and produce flowers at a height of only six inches.

The delight in viewing daffodils on the lawn must be compensated for by enduring the unsightly foliage while it is dying down and feeding the bulbs for next year's blooming. Daffodils are hardy but it doesn't make sense to spend money for bulbs and then defeat their growth pattern by shearing off the leaves as soon as the golden trumpets begin to fade.

The daffodils now blooming by my low stone wall are all survivors from a clump of tightly clustered leaves I discovered in the field near the old barn. Too tightly grown to bloom, they were recognizable as part of the narcissus family. This is their second year since the rescue, separation, and replanting. They are rewarding me with cheerful blooms about ten inches high and seem responsive to the space and compost feedings so that each one is ready to divide into bulbs for future springs.

Blossoming with the daffodils is the purplish-blue *Mertensia virginica*, which the wildflower book lists as Virginia cowslip, and *Arabis albida* or wall cress with miniature spikes of white. The books say the *Mertensia virginica* needs moist shaded soil but I didn't read that until three years after I had discovered the plant among weeds in a neglected garden and transplanted it into about the sunniest spot in my border. It's a reliable spring-blooming perennial and the only trouble I have is remembering to mark where it grows. In June it dies down and disappears. If I forget where it lives and dig to set in summer blooming plants, the Virginia cowslip roots can be damaged or destroyed.

Yellow daffodils are striking against the lush green lawn. They're cheerful and effective among the purple and white blooms in my border. But next year I think I'd like to see a double ring of golden daffodils around the one surviving elm tree in the east field. Enough to make a strong showing—planted in random order—with perhaps a bit of the purplish cowslip for contrast.

New varieties of daffodils—hybridized both in this country and in England and Holland—can be chosen for early blooming, late blooming, and a bit of in between so that the bright trumpet flowers will prolong the pleasure they bring.

There's a legend that the first "mail-order" brides, who gambled their future and came from England to Jamestown to marry the men who held the fort, brought narcissus bulbs in their pockets. Certainly other brides, heading west to new homesteads, tucked spring bulbs into their baggage. From the Hudson River Valley to the tidewaters of the Columbia, flat jonquils and ruffled daffodils added brightness to springtime. Today Oregon seems to be the leader in commercial bulb growing—shipping these good fortune symbols back east to brighten our May gardens.

LUSH IS THE WORD which comes to mind in looking at my lawn this week. The rich greenness is like the foggy fields of Ireland. The luxuriant growth—especially where I spread the sheep manure last fall—tempts me to trip barefooted across the damp and springy turf.

I could moan about the rapid growth since I haven't yet had the lawnmower repaired or groan about the number of square yards which need leveling. But there's a lilt in the breeze and joy in the green growth which even the black flies don't diminish. My peas are under water, and this isn't what the garden book means by their needing damp, cool soil. However, May is no time for mewling. There's too much to enjoy.

The Johnny-jump-ups are blooming in every corner of the garden where they could find a bit of uncovered soil in which to propagate themselves. These early bloomers always turn their tiny cheerful blossoms toward the sun. Also known as ladies' delights, heartease and wild pansy, these hardy violas resemble miniature pansies and grow in many color variations. Last year after I had pulled out bushels of them (tossed onto the compost), I found the grocery stores were selling wee flats of much weaker plants for $1.39.

The new strawberry bed—low on the east end of the garden—and the old bed—high on the west—wintered well and more green leaves are puffing out every day. I suppose this would be the year to try the middle soil for raising berries but the thought of plowing under all the plants in my first bed is one I'm not ready to face quite yet. I think some wild strawberries have mingled in with the purchased plants, and I want to learn more about identifying while these are here to observe.

It's the learning by doing which is one of the big pluses of backyard gardening. Even if I didn't like eggplant, I think I'd grow a few just to see the purple blossoms and the way the fruits develop from jelly bean-size to fat shiny globes ready for ratatouille, moussaka, or eggplant Parmesan. Watching kohlrabi develop into round, edible, spaceship-looking vegetables and picking purple beans are also viewing pleasures.

An older neighbor used to raise celery—fat, full bunches, evenly blanched and full of flavor. He never ate any—claimed he'd as soon taste iodine—but he did "admire to see it grow." This gardener also raised melons, adapting his cultivation methods to the neighborhood poultry industry of those years. Wherever truckloads of hen manure had been dumped in the nearby fields, he'd dig a hole, fill it with soil and plant melon seeds. The heat of the pile got them off to an early start and apparently kept them thriving.

In July, old Tom would cut off the vine ends and carve initials in the growing fruits. By late August he was ready to harvest and deliver and what neighbor could refuse a ripe, round melon wearing his monogram?

In addition to the pleasure of watching plants grow and the exercise in the fresh air while gardening, the flavor and texture of garden-fresh food cannot be purchased in any market. Store vegetables are usually produce raised from seeds of plants developed to be extra firm to withstand the commercial harvesting, shipping and sorting. Cabbages tough enough to be kicked to market and still arrive in salable condition can be purchased in every state, but the tender sweetness of an early Jersey Wakefield is best ten minutes from the backyard garden. Sliced or chopped, it's a delightful snack to munch on while reading.

Head lettuce has its merits, but for true lettuce flavor the fragile leaves of home-grown loose leaf varieties are best. Country folks often consume bowls full of lettuce leaves dipped in vinegar and sprinkled with sugar. By planting about ten seeds each Sunday morning from Easter until Labor Day, there should be fresh lettuce available for all the family salads and sandwiches.

The seedlings in the guest room are developing a jungle-like look. The kitchen counters have sorted seed packets somewhat organized into a planting time plan, and the new garden books are stacked by the wing chairs. The rains which are bringing that lushness to my lawns have not dampened my gardening spirits.

There's a genuine physical pleasure in the manipulation of the soil and—when the weather isn't right—a lift and lightness of spirit in just contemplating the coming of another growing season. Even the revival of the weeds seems to remind me of the tremendous potential of life. May is a month of promise.

RHUBARB

We know that spring has really come to the Georges River valley when there are two rhubarb pies for dinner—the traditional old-fashioned kind flavored with a bit of grated orange peel and our own Sennebec Hill rhubarb custard pie with a sprinkling of freshly ground nutmeg.

Before this, when the first pink shoots appear, we enjoy sunny hours re-mulching the twenty-seven hills of rhubarb and adding fertilizer for the coming year. The winter's accumulation of magazines and newspapers are lavishly spread between the rows; handfuls of a 5–10–10 commercial fertilizer are scattered about to speed the breakdown of the paper; and the whole plot is covered heavily with bales of hay that had banked the farmhouse during the winter. One pail of well-rotted manure dumped on each hill and we are ready for another year—a year of eating, freezing, selling, and inventing new recipes to use up the indefatigable bounty of rhubarb.

New England provides the ideal climate for growing rhubarb, and according to John Lowell, one of the founders of the Massachusetts Horticultural Society, it was a Maine gardener who introduced rhubarb into America as a food plant. The history of rhubarb covers almost forty-seven centuries, going back to 2700 B.C. in China. Cultivated as a medicine for use as a purgative and a gastric tonic, roots at least five years old were sliced, dried, and then powdered. Early travelers carried the plant from China to Persia, Greece, and Russia; it was grown in the early botanical gardens at Padua, Italy, taken to England and Scotland, and then to America.

The garden journals of George Washington, John Jay, and Thomas Jefferson record their planting of rhubarb, and in

1770 Benjamin Franklin sent rhubarb seeds from Scotland to his botanist friend, John Bartram. But it wasn't until about 1780 that recipe books began to mention its use in tarts and pies. Probably because sugar was a scarce commodity in rural New England, it was after 1800 that rhubarb gained the Yankee name "pieplant." Brides going forth to newly cleared acres took along a crock of sourdough yeast, a few cuttings of lilac, and a clump of rhubarb roots. And Lewis and Clark carried powdered rhubarb root on their journey of exploration to the Pacific.

While icy northern winters killed fruit trees, the pieplant seldom failed to furnish the first fresh food each spring. Out on Matinicus Island, a clump set out by Iddo Tolman in 1858 is still growing, requiring only occasional fertilizing to nourish the crisp, tart stalks that are one of the culinary joys of the spring season.

Rhubarb needs to be planted in a place apart, where it will not be disturbed for years, and it needs full sun for at least half of each day. Healthy, well-fed rhubarb is a handsome plant and when set against a stone wall or the base of a shed or barn, the great spreading leaves fan out like rainforest vegetation. Rows of rhubarb can be set as a border between lawn and garden.

If you're buying rhubarb roots, MacDonald, Valentine, and Chipman's Canada Red are recommended varieties. But it isn't necessary to be fussy. The quickest way to start a bed is to beg a few roots from a neighbor. Since the plants need to be divided or thinned about every six years, most rhubarb growers will cheerfully give you enough to start your hills.

The roots should be dug and divided before the first leaves begin to uncurl in May. Spade up a clump and hose away the soil so you can easily cut the root mass apart, leaving one bud on each new division. Plant the roots three feet apart with the buds set about two inches below the soil surface. Because a rhubarb bed is usually a lifetime investment, the roots should be set in good loam enriched with compost and old manure. But because rhubarb is such a hardy plant it will do well in almost any soil as long as there is good drainage and as long as it is fed annually with plenty of old hay or compost. Many rhubarb growers feed their plants by dumping kitchen scraps—peelings and other compost materials—right under the spreading leaves.

There's a local story about a coastal farmer who once asked a neighbor for enough rhubarb for a bit of sauce. Upon being told that there was none to spare, the farmer promptly went out and acquired enough roots to plant a two-hundred-foot row. He allowed as how no one would ever ask *him* for a mite of rhubarb without being generously provided. Years later, when a younger man took over the farm, the roots needed dividing. With true Yankee ingenuity, the young fellow drove his plow straight down the middle of the whole row, split the plants in half, transplanted one part, filled in the furrow, and ended up with two two-hundred-foot rows.

I once read that farmers in Afghanistan cover their rhubarb with several feet of gravel so that by the time the shoots have struggled up through this, they are pale and very tender. By placing a chimney tile over one of my plants and pouring several pails of sand inside it, I have produced a reasonably accurate facsimile of this method and found the stalks far more delicate than those of the usual plant. Another year I discovered a way to produce earlier rhubarb: placing an open-ended barrel over one hill and mounding manure up around the outside of it, I got tender ruby stalks weeks ahead of the rhubarb in the open field.

The best rhubarb for cooking, canning, or freezing comes from the long tender stalks of well-fed roots pulled between May 1 and July 4. After that the skin gets tougher (although a well-mulched bed will produce good stalks for pie as late as August). One of our favorites is blu-barb pie, half blueberry and half rhubarb, invented in 1962 for the Maine Blueberry Festival.

Although rhubarb is a vegetable, it is generally used as a fruit—naturally enough, since it is in season in spring when fresh fruits are scarce. Because it's easy to freeze, it can provide a variety of desserts all through a winter.

Rhubarb should be pulled—not cut. Stalks should be twisted sideways and pulled at an angle. Snip the leaves and the base of the stems onto the mulch around the plants. To freeze rhubarb, wash, dry, cut into half-inch pieces, spread on a cookie sheet, and freeze. In this way it is possible to take out any amount needed for a recipe. Double plastic bags are easiest for packaging.

Old-timers around this part of Maine claim that rhubarb has a tranquilizing effect and surely almost anyone would agree that a flaky-crusted rhubarb pie can exert a calming effect at the end of a working day. But rhubarb is versatile and can be used in many ways.

SENNEBEC HILL RHUBARB PIE

Beat together:

1 1/2 cups sugar   2 tablespoons butter
2 eggs   1/4 cup flour
1/2 teaspoon nutmeg   1/2 teaspoon salt

Stir into this: 3 cups cut rhubarb (smaller pieces blend better). Use as a filling for a two-crust pie. Bake 10 minutes at 450°; 40 minutes at 350°.

BLU-BARB PIE

Mix together:

1 cup sugar (1⅓ if you prefer sweeter desserts)
¼ cup flour
¼ teaspoon salt

1½ cups rhubarb cut in small pieces
1½ cups blueberries (fresh or frozen)

Dot with bits of butter.

Bake as a two-crust pie, 10 minutes at 450° and 30 minutes at 350°.

RHUBARB RAISIN PIE

3 cups finely cut rhubarb
1¼ cups sugar
2 tablespoons flour
1 egg slightly beaten

½ cup raisins
¼ teaspoon salt
1 tablespoon butter

Mix together and bake as a two-crust pie. Bake at 450° for 10 minutes; 30 minutes at 375°.

STRAWBERRY RHUBARD PIE

Blend together:

2 cups cut rhubarb
2 cups sliced strawberries
1¼ cups sugar

¼ teaspoon salt
⅓ cup flour
2 tablespoons butter

Bake as a two-crust pie at 450° for 10 minutes and 30 minutes at 375°.

Rhubarb Flummery

4 cups cut rhubarb
1¾ cups sugar
Stew gently for 10 minutes.

8 slices of buttered white
bread

Layer buttered bread and warm stewed rhubarb in a deep baking dish. Chill for 24 hours. Serve with whipped cream flavored with freshly ground nutmeg.

Baked Rhubarb

1 pound makes 2 cups
cooked

Use 1 cup of sugar to 2
cups rhubarb

Cut washed rhubarb into inch-long pieces. Cover with sugar in a casserole. Let stand for 1 hour. Bake for 1 hour at 325°.

Rhubarb Cake

This is ideal for summer picnics. Can be made and frozen in June.

½ cup sugar

2 cups finely cut rhubarb

Mix and set aside.
Blend together:
½ cup butter
1½ cups sugar

1 egg
1 teaspoon vanilla

Mix together:

2 cups plus 2 tablespoons
flour

1 teaspoon cinnamon

1 teaspoon baking soda

½ teaspoon salt

Add alternately to blended mixture with 1 cup buttermilk or sour milk. Add rhubarb mixture.

Add:

½ cup shredded coconut

½ cup raisins

½ cup chopped walnuts or
pecans

Blend together. Pour into a greased and floured 7- by 12-inch pan. Bake at 350° for 45 minutes.

Sennebec Pudding

Mix together:

2 cups blueberries (fresh or
frozen)

1½ cups cut rhubarb (fresh
or frozen)

1 teaspoon tapioca

1¼ cups sugar

Put this mixture into a buttered 2-quart casserole.

Mix together:

½ cup sugar

½ cup flour

½ cup oatmeal

¼ wheat germ

Blend in ¼ cup butter

Spread over fruit mixture. Bake 45 minutes at 350°. Serve warm with vanilla ice cream.

THE GREEN PATTERN has begun. Watching the earth come to life around the pond each year I marvel at the multitude of shades of green. In a living room or in a quilt they would be jarring and ugly. Spread out through the valley they blend in beauty.

This pulsing panorama of springtime growth tends to stimulate me and many other gardeners to expand and over-extend in planting. Here hindsight can be a handy garden tool. Last August was a good time to be realistic about the pleasures of summer gardening and the fresh produce I was actually using and enjoying. It was also a time to measure and count. Those notes on the amount of space one cabbage fills, the number of pepper plants needed to supply the twelve quarts I wanted for freezer and for pickles, and the actual amount of lettuce cut from a ten-foot row are being used now to temper my May enthusiasm.

Rotation of crops—even in a small kitchen garden—is a kind of insurance. Most important is exchanging spaces of root crops and above-the-ground edibles. My onions are now planted where the string beans grew last year. The beans will go in where beets grew last summer. A garden plan on graph paper or garden photos will help in planning regular rotation.

Cabbages get enormous. By the first of August some are as big as washtubs. But each year when I begin to set the tender little plants into the ground, it's difficult to remember and to visualize the space they will fill. However, my notes remind me that my perception has been faulty in the past and give the actual measurements of last year's crop. So, using the lid of a large garbage can like a cookie cutter, I press a circle in the soil, outline it with lime and thus mark out a double staggered row.

The young cabbages look small and lonely set in those circles so I plant radishes or spinach around them. These will be full-grown and harvested before the cabbages stretch out (as they will) to fill the full circles.

Giving careful thought to spacing during spring planting will make the summer care of a garden easier. My own preference is to give up as little space as possible to paths or walks. This means less garden soil getting compacted and less rows to hoe. Single rows seem downright unsociable and wasteful. Three rows of beans, staggered in a zig-zag grouping, help to hold each other up in case of high winds. With one section four feet by six feet, it's easy to weed and to pick. If watering is necessary, little is wasted running off into garden walks.

Carrots and beets (and other root crops) need loose, well-aerated soil. The addition of sand when the garden has heavy clay soil and the addition of lime or wood ashes and compost will give the roots a chance to grow with ease. By the time I have spaded these ingredients into an area in my garden, I have a raised bed, again about four feet by six feet. Since raised beds warm up more quickly in the spring and drain off excess water in the fall, this way of growing carrots and beets works well. When the surface has been raked smooth, I scatter plant the seeds. Carrot seeds mixed with dried coffee grounds will scatter more evenly—or at least it's possible to see where they aren't even and, with an old fork, rake them into a more regular distribution.

When the seeds have been covered with about one quarter inch of soil, it is most important to press the surface to be sure each tiny seed is in firm contact with the surrounding earth. I place a wide board across the bed and walk across it. If there's no traffic, I sometimes dance a jig while humming a fertility tune. By moving the board and repeating the ritual, I can expect better germination. A light dusting of sawdust, old manure, or a cover of burlap will prevent the bed from drying out before the tiny seeds sprout.

May think-aheads pay dividends in August and September. Consider the wind direction in your garden before setting in the pepper plants (when it's warm enough). Unless they are protected by other sturdier plants, the peppers will tip over or use up so much energy trying to grow that they won't produce. Planting all the fall crops—the ones you'll be eating out of the garden in October—in one end of the garden will make harvesting and clean-ups more convenient. Chard, kale and leeks will supply fresh eating after many a frost. Clumps of annuals as row markers or dividers will be a joy to view blooming brightly among the greens. Petunias and snapdragons flower into November.

Rotating the planting of any kitchen garden will help in keeping the soil healthy, but the soil needs to be fed. Compost and old sawdust and grass clippings add tilth. Manure, good year-old manure, sets the organisms of the soil to celebrating spring. I wonder if any of my thoughtful children will once again send me a dump truck load of manure as a Mother's Day gift?

WHEN ANNA JARVIS decided that too many grown children were thoughtless and neglectful of their mothers, she started a one-woman campaign for a special day on which all offspring would pay homage to their maternal parent. Her unrelenting letter-writing was successful and in May, 1914 President Woodrow Wilson issued a proclamation inviting "the people of the U.S. to display the flag at their homes or other suitable places on the second Sunday of May as a public expression of our love and reverence for the mothers of this country."

Poor Miss Jarvis. She never did become a mother herself and for thirty-four years she watched what she had expected to be a religious observance become a commercial holiday exploited by manufacturers and the advertising world. The myth that every successfully fertilized female blossomed into a wise, patient, understanding and loving mother was promoted. All the hidden strings of guilt were twanged to head the public toward the cash registers.

Miss Jarvis didn't live to hear the sweet thirty-second TV Mother's Day messages produced at a cost of $80,000 to $200,000 and run between the news broadcasts of latest statistics on teenage pregnancies and child abuse. If all the money spent on gifts and gift promotions for this one Sunday in the year was spent for planned parenthood clinics and counseling centers, would it result in changing the evening news statistics?

Flying flags as a public expression of love and appreciation isn't a bad idea, but why does it have to be ritualized and done on one day in May? After eighteen years of teaching twelve- and thirteen-year-olds and meeting their parents, I know there should be flags flying from some rooftops every day. I cherish a note one mother sent with a bouquet of flowers. "Someday our son will be a delightful, responsible adult. But right now he's thirteen and we've had a long rainy weekend. Thinking of you shut up in there with seventy of these, I'm sending flowers."

A friend of mine used to say that if adults had to pass a test before being allowed by law to have children, it would cut down on population and problems. Perhaps. But who would devise the test? Being a parent seems to be a learn-along-the-way job and probably no other endeavor forces adults to change and grow the way twenty-four-hour constant parenthood does.

The Good Mommy as seen on television never seems to have an infant who cries with colic half the night nor a toddler adept at house-wrecking just before the Good Daddy comes home to shiny waxed floors, a gourmet dinner, and a scented, smiling spouse. Certainly the TV image mother doesn't shriek "How did I get into this?"

If the media visions of what a happy family should be like aren't enough to stir up guilt feelings, there are all the relatives and neighbors hinting or suggesting that your little ones could do with a bit of better parenting. And the left-over admonitions from one's own childhood. Unrealistic expectations cloud the family scene.

Perhaps Mother's Day—while spring is changing the natural world in a rush of glorious growth—might be a good time to face the fact that there are no perfect parents and probably never will be. It might be a good time to list and crow about the good things which have been part of parenting and are still taking place, to relax and listen to the kids and be grateful that you've all survived. And to let go of some of the admonitions about the Good Mommies which may have been true in 1900 but don't mesh with today's rising percentage of single-parent families.

The myths of motherhood keep turning up in advertising. They stir uneasy feelings which need to be dispelled by taking a look from a different perspective. When I drive by Chickawaukee Pond, I wonder why it wasn't called Fecundity.

There's a motherhood story. Back when Isaiah Tolman settled by those waters, it was known as Tolman Pond. When his first wife died after bearing eight children, he certainly needed someone to mother his brood. Wife number two played the Good Mommy by 1700 rules and didn't die until she'd added eleven little Tolmans and Isaiah had to find another wife to help with parenting. She bore him two children. Seventeen of those twenty-one children survived and none of those mothers were bombarded by commercial advice and sentimentality. Are we being two hundred years smarter?

IF ONLY MAY could be put "on hold!" Before there's time to admire the pastel colors of the budding trees across the pond, they're bursting into full leaf and the soft differences of shading merge toward summer green.

Every day, every hour, something grows an inch. The asparagus pushes its spears up so fast I can see it grow. The rhubarb burgeons into overlapping clumps and the crabapple tree races the pear trees into bloom. Twenty-four hours after the lawn has been mowed another set of bold, gold blossoms decorates the green.

Even the black flies—clouds of blood-hungry gnats—can't spoil the magnificence of May. I retreat to the house after each attack and then return to work where some bit of breeze will disrupt their flight patterns. A southern gentleman experiencing his first Maine spring inquired about how long these biting pests lasted. A Maine-born man told him about three weeks. A five-year resident answered about two months, while a fisherman and gardener suggested that they're usually gone by August 4, if there are enough mosquitoes to take over. Maybe we just get accustomed to them?

The rampant growth of May is underground, as well as in the foliage and the perennials I'm trying to identify and then move, thrusting roots out and down. They'll soon be past the stage for successful transplanting. Most of these plants—delphiniums, phlox, day lilies, Maltese cross—need a space as big as the lid of a garbage can and they need to get growing in May. And May is racing by.

When my first two children were small, we had a project called "Lovely Park" out behind the shed where it wouldn't interfere with all the proper farm activities. I built a compost bin and we planted around it. When we found a plant we liked on our woods walks, we'd dig it up and put it in our park. Sometimes they survived and we could find them in the books and learn the names.

Somewhere I had read that calendulas were easy to grow,

so we bought a package of seeds. I still refer to calendulas as "moron flowers" because anyone can grow them. The kids and I transplanted them. There were no "don't touch" rules in that small space and we learned together. The three of us were equal in our knowledge of country living and growing plants.

By the time child number three was big enough to toddle through the gardens, the first two were becoming experts at identifying tiny seedlings as weeds, calendulas, or spinach. Then the shed had to be torn down—crashing upon Lovely Park—and our project was buried in debris. But the seeds of pleasure in growing survived and gardening is part of all of our lives today.

In the midst of the rush of growth in May—the constant change and resurgent life—being in the garden working in the earth brings a fresh sense of the rhythm of the whole universe. I can plant seeds and cultivate but the life within that seed is quite beyond my control. May is a glorious month on our calendar but it's the calendar of the earth, the sun, and the stars which determines the growth.

The seedlings on the dining room table and kitchen counters are ready for another transplanting and thinning and then the days of hardening off before being set out in full sun. The Siberian tomatoes—sent from a fellow gardener in Canada—are racing my Sennebec orange tomato seedlings. The Pick-Me-Quick peppers I'm testing for Gurney's are sturdier but not taller than the Gypsy peppers which won an All-American Selections award in 1981. Just watching the daily changes is a welcome part of spring.

But meanwhile out in the kitchen garden the black flies are convening to feast upon me while I'm trying to spade up the beds for these seedlings. Last year's garden plan will be reversed. What was planted on the north side will grow this year on the south side of the center path.

May's growth pattern extends to grass and weeds. What

were bits of green last week are clumps of rooted plants now. The Johnny-jump-ups in six different color patterns are blossoming all over the edges of the garden and the starburst leaves of wild radishes are clustered along the strawberries.

May is bright and beautiful with an urgency of growth. It's a month of color and change and promise. I'd like more time to be out in this surging world here on my own acres. But since nature won't wait, I'll look forward to lilacs and apple blossoms and the first red rhubarb pie.

LONG AGO in a mystery, a New England suspense story, I found a reference to lilacs as markers of old cellar holes. The city-bred heroine pursued by the murderer took to the woods and cowered behind a clump of flowering lilacs. The villain, allergic to bees, was stung and perished miserably beside the cornerstone of an old stone foundation. The story ended with all the threads tied up but left me with the question, "If the farm buildings had competely disintegrated, would the lilacs still bloom?"

Since moving to Maine, driving along back roads and hiking over long discontinued roadways have provided ample proof of the hardiness and tenacity of this flowering shrub. Rampant purple blossoms along wooded roads, visible among the soft greens of trees leafing out in May, do indeed indicate old cellar holes. Glimpses of purple have led to the discovery of overgrown graveyards.

Cutting lilacs was a spring ritual when the children were young. An abandoned farm up the road was lavish with lilacs, and we could cut armfuls and have bouquets in every room. A lovely old gray pickle crock was the right container for a living room display. We hadn't read about the superstitions associated with lilacs or with purple. We enjoyed. It was pleasant to waken to a fragrant house.

New Englanders once believed that purple hues should not be permitted indoors. These symbolized mourning and sadness and might bring bad luck. Young women were reminded, "She who wears lilacs will never wear a wedding ring." Sending a bouquet of lilacs was a way of telling one's betrothed of a wish to break off an engagement. Related, perhaps, to "In the spring a young man's fancy . . ."

Blooming early and bountifully after winter in a climate where winters are cold—for lilacs will grow as far north as Hudson Bay—this shrub was once planted beside almost every New England home. And, come spring, looking for a five-corolla-lobed lilac, like seeking a four-leaf clover, was supposed to bring good luck. As long as the purple blossoms remained in the dooryard.

The word lilac comes from a Persian term for "bluish" but plant historians believe this hardy shrub was brought from the mountain slopes of southwestern China. Since only prized possessions warranted inclusion in the burden of the long caravan journeys, the lilac's transplanting suggests that its fragrant early blooming has pleasured man's sense of beauty for centuries.

By the seventeenth century lilacs were a favorite in Europe and were blooming in both castle and cottage gardens in England. New Hampshire may have been the site of the first lilacs planted in America, and this is their state flower. In 1750 when Benning Wentworth, colonial governor of New Hampshire, laid out a terrace to complete his rambling fifty-two-room mansion, he had lilacs brought from England.

Governor Wentworth is remembered for the beauty of his lilac shrubbery, and since he entertained often and sumptuously, his guests copied his landscaping and spring blossoms of this shrub spread up and down the New England countryside.

Wentworth is also remembered for his impulsive second marriage. After his guests had enjoyed the dinner celebrating his sixtieth birthday, Wentworth ordered the rector of St. John's Church in Portsmouth to marry him then and there to his beautiful servant, Martha Hilton, who had just turned twenty. Martha Wentworth inherited the coastal estate and entertained George Washington there. And some references state that the second lilacs imported to America were planted at Mount Vernon.

In England the lilac was sometimes called the "pipe-tree" because the stems of pipes could be easily formed from lilac wood and a few tales suggest that the great god Pan used hollow lilac shoots instead of river reeds for the musical pipes which enticed maidens into the spring woodlands.

When Decoration Day was planned as a nationwide observance in 1868 for the purpose of strewing flowers or otherwise decorating the graves of those who died in defense of their country during the Civil War, New England had lilacs in bloom upon that May date.

And we still do. Although I've heard that Rochester, N.Y. has to hold its Lilac Festival some years without the purple blooms because of nasty spring weather, local lilacs seem to demonstrate their hardiness and tenacity. The color may symbolize mourning, but the fragrant blooms proclaim renewal, the strength of the life force.

ASPARAGUS

Halfway down the hill, between the farmhouse and the pond, in full sun, is the best asparagus bed in Knox County, Maine— luxuriant proof that nature is often kind to bungling ama-teurs. If I were to do it again I'd do it right. Instead, I give free advice to friends and neighbors, letting them profit from my trials and errors, and even supply them with seedlings so they can begin to raise this first crop of the season.

I never intended to start an asparagus bed. In fact, I had never seen one. But one sunny May morning, on my way down to swim, I paused to enjoy three bobolinks trying to out-sing each other and saw, pushing up through the tangled mesh of witch grass, one spear of asparagus. The taste was delicious, and because it was pleasant there in the spring sunshine, I began to tug at the tough grass in search of another.

Every day before swimming I spent a few minutes wrestling with the witch grass and eventually uncovered eight aspar-agus plants, weak and undernourished but determined to survive. Then, to prevent the grass and weeds from covering the plants again, I began to bring up from the pond pails of the pulverized leaves that storms toss up along the beach. A few minutes each day kept the shore tidy and the asparagus well mulched.

A friend gave me a few roots so I could see what they looked like. It seemed incredible that sixty or more fat, juicy, green spears could be produced by such pale, dry, octopus-shaped things. If I had realized then that each of these would grow hundreds more root shoots, fat and fleshy, extending downward six or eight feet and that a mature plant would occupy more than a hundred cubic feet, I would have done more than just spade up a small spot and lay them in.

Since an asparagus bed is going to provide nourishment for twenty years, it makes sense to prepare the soil well. The more nutrients you can put into the original trench, down where the roots will be seeking it, the better your roots can produce. Once the plants are set in, you can only feed them from the top, depending upon rains and earthworms to carry the plant food down to where it is needed.

Twelve asparagus plants, I discovered, were an aggravation. Anyone who likes asparagus—and it's currently rated as the fifth most popular vegetable in America—needs ten or twelve plants for each family member.

The year I discovered the asparagus, a new language program was started in the school where I teach. Each of my seventy students was expected to complete a nice, fat workbook before the end of May. Like many educational programs that are cheerfully promoted by those who do not have to be shut up in a classroom with dozens of resistant students, this one generated animated animosity. By the time we had suffered through to the final pages, the workbooks—inside and out—contained a fine collection of graffiti expressing the students' feelings. Some celebration seemed necessary.

So we marched the bedraggled, never-to-be-used-again books out to my car and I promised to bury them near the manure pile. Slave labor was promptly volunteered. The students who came out to the farm enthusiastically labored at lugging the workbooks down the hill, laying them out along the sides of my new asparagus bed and over the area where I planned to extend the bed. Then we covered the workbooks liberally with hay. During the summer months when students stopped by to swim, they always made a pilgrimage to the asparagus bed to lift the hay and gloat over the decay of the detested pages.

By the next spring the earthworms had industriously demolished most of the heavy sod and reduced the language workbooks to compost. I was able to dig a trench and set out my new asparagus roots.

If I were to do it again, I would not dig a trench—especially with the constant company of nine hundred blackflies; I would have one dug. At least, I would have a deep furrow plowed. And I would have it dug or plowed in the fall, because the soil is often too wet in the spring to prepare a trench. By starting with a trench twelve or fifteen inches deep and the same width, you can build a bed of rich soil. Asparagus is a heavy feeder and requires heavy applications of liming materials. Starting at the bottom where it can go to work more readily, add twenty pounds of pulverized lime-stone and three pounds of superphosphate for every one hundred square feet.

Next, add three or four inches of well-rotted manure. Walk up and down the trench a few times and tamp this down before adding good loam. If your soil is poor, buy enough loam to complete the project properly. Price asparagus in the market and estimate your future production. Economically, as you'll see, it's a sound investment.

When I dug my trench I discovered that the glacier that had carved out this valley had apparently hiccupped on this hillside and deposited a mess of rocks. The asparagus plants now growing where I hauled in good top soil produce five times as many spears as those that were just tucked into the existing soil.

Most people start an asparagus bed by buying year-old roots. These should be ordered early and planted immediately after they have been soaked overnight. Order more roots than you plan to set out so that you can discard any that are weak or damaged.

A twenty foot strip in your vegetable garden will produce all the seedlings you will need for your permanent trench and since asparagus is easy to raise from seed, this is probably the best way to start a really good bed. This way, you know that your plants never will be crowded, dried out, or damaged. You'll get better roots because you can lift them from their growing row and reset them into the prepared trench with no chance of drying or bruising, no loss of vitality. The seed of the asparagus is large and black and slow to germinate. Soaking the seeds overnight before planting and keeping the row well watered will promote germination, since moisture is most essential to proper growth.

Asparagus plants have long roots and, as soon as the crown begins to form, they branch out in all directions. For this reason the seeds should be planted about four inches apart to eliminate thinning later. In trying to pull out the unwanted or crowded shoots, you'll find that they often break off at the crown and then sprout again. The resulting tangle inhibits strong growth, and the roots can be injured when you try to separate them.

I dig a shallow trench with a hoe—about one and one-half inches deep and just the width of the hoe. Then I take a roll of toilet tissue and roll it out so that one layer covers the full length of the row. I can easily see the seeds on the paper and can avoid planting them too closely. When the seeds are covered with soil, I water well. The paper soon disintegrates and becomes part of the soil. (In New England the best time to sow asparagus seeds seems to be the week the apple blossoms' petals begin to drift across your garden.)

The seedlings need to be kept well weeded and well watered. A side dressing of a 5–10–5 fertilizer should be dug in— carefully—when the sprouts are about four inches high. By September the top growth—the ferns—should be about three feet high. These new roots should be left in place until the following spring, when they will be set into the permanent trench. Choose only the largest and strongest ones for transplanting.

Whether you buy year-old roots or plan to transplant those you raised from seed, set them into the permanent bed as early in the spring as your soil is ready—that is, when a handful crumbles easily instead of lumping. Set each plant no more than five inches below the surface and space them a full eighteen inches apart. Spread each root out carefully so that it can reach in all directions and cover at once with two inches of soil. Water well. The object is to grow roots that are as long and as strong as possible and to do this they must be kept moist.

As the roots begin to sprout and send up spears in the permanent trench, rake in a little topsoil each week (too much too soon may smother them). By fall, the soil level in the trench should be that of the area surrounding it.

Next you need restraint. Not one spear should be cut until the second year after the roots have been planted in the permanent bed. Cutting too many spears the second year can weaken the plants. But after that, if the bed is well limed and fertilized twice a year—in April and July—you can feast on one of the most delicious of vegetables. And, if you've never eaten asparagus just fifteen minutes from the garden, you don't really know the flavor of this spring crop.

Asparagus should be cut when the spears are eight inches high *or* when the tips begin to unfurl—whichever comes first. The harvesting season here in New England should end on the Fourth of July: then the spears are allowed to grow into ferns. From the ferns the roots build up the store of food needed to produce the next year's crop. These ferns should not be cut off until late in the fall since they will feed the roots until frost. In October when I cut mine, I leave the stalks about four inches high. Then, in the spring, I can easily see where each root is and avoid stepping where the first tender spears may be growing.

Weed control in an asparagus bed is most important. Since a heavy mulch prevents the growth of weeds, while furnishing extra nutrients to the roots, this seems the most efficient way to care for an asparagus bed. I swim twice a day from May until mid-October and stop in the asparagus bed for a few minutes each day on my way down the hill. A few minutes' care every day instead of several back-breaking hours several times a year makes asparagus culture a joy instead of a burden. In this way, I pull out weeds, scoop out any sprouting seedlings, which could grow and smother the mature, producing roots, and prune out weak or broken stalks. This daily survey keeps me aware of the changes in foliage color and the possible need for extra or different fertilizers, or the need for extra watering.

On my way back from swimming, I carry up two pails of what we call "lake mulch." This is composed of the leaves that fall into the pond each fall and are ground, smashed, and pulverized into a fine flaky organic material—in abundance. Four pails per day keep the whole seventy feet of the asparagus bed fed and protected from weeds.

An extra-heavy mulch separates my asparagus bed from the surrounding fields, where milkweed threatens to take over the earth. Each June I bring home school workbooks, posters, and left-over art work—especially the six-foot-long murals. They are spread along the sides of the bed and covered with hay.

The only problem I've had with mulching is from slugs. Since these creatures can't stand to have their bellies scratched, I mix sand, limestone, and salt, and spread a two-inch-wide line of this along the edge of the hay mulch. I believe the old line: "Salt on its tail will kill any snail."

Long before asparagus was used for food it had a reputation along the Mediterranean as a nostrum for almost anything, from the prevention of bee stings to heart trouble, dropsy, and toothache. Now, twenty centuries later, a "no-aging" diet recommends eating asparagus three times a week because of its nucleic acid content.

Asparagus is at its best fresh from the garden, cooked no more than six minutes and served, well drained, with melted butter. Because it freezes well, this vegetable can be a family treat all year. Besides what we eat and sell, my seventy-foot row produces enough to freeze twenty pounds a year. I blanch asparagus for two minutes, cool in ice water, drain *very* well on old white towels, and freeze on cookie sheets. Then I pack it in double plastic bags. Because the stalks aren't stuck together, any amount desired can be removed for a meal.

I freeze my spears in six-inch lengths because that size fits into my favorite cooking pan. The trimmings are then sliced diagonally, blanched, chilled, drained, and frozen to be used as greens in Chinese dishes. For the end-of-school faculty picnic I make a casserole of eight cups of asparagus cut into two-inch pieces, cooked five minutes in chicken broth, mixed with two cups of cubed cooked turkey and two cans of mushrooms.

The best asparagus bed in Knox County, Maine, started quite by accident, but for ten years it has provided gastronomical pleasures and, to date, has provided enough seedlings for seven more families to have their own asparagus beds and enjoy this most succulent of spring vegetables.

ASPARAGUS DINNER PIE

1 baked 9 inch pie shell
1½ pounds of asparagus
(about 4 cups)
½ cup shredded Swiss
cheese
¼ cup minced or slivered
ham
5 hard-boiled eggs

3 tablespoons butter
3 tablespoons flour
1 cup milk
1 chicken bouillon cube
1 teaspoon instant minced
onion
Salt and pepper

Cook asparagus in small amount of water until just tender—about 6 minutes or less. Drain.

Melt butter, stir in flour until smooth, and add milk gradually, stirring until well-blended. Cook, stirring constantly, until sauce thickens. Stir in crushed bouillon cube, onion, salt and pepper and stir until bouillon is dissolved.

Chop 3 of the eggs and stir into sauce. Place the drained asparagus into pie shell. Spread ham over this. Cover with sauce and spread cheese on top.

Bake at 350 degrees until cheese melts. Garnish with slices of other 2 hard-boiled eggs.

Turkey Roll-ups

Cook frozen or fresh asparagus until just tender. Slice turkey breast into enough for at least two slices per person.

Place 2 or 3 asparagus spears on each slice of turkey. Roll and place seam side down in a buttered baking pan.

Heat together and stir until smooth:
1 can of condensed cream of onion soup
½ cup milk

½ teaspoon Worcestershire sauce
¼ cup shredded sharp cheese

Cover turkey rolls with sauce and bake until bubbly hot. Or—cover turkey rolls with foil and heat them in the oven and spoon hot sauce over them before serving.

ASPARAGUS SALAD

Cook and drain 2 pounds of asparagus cut and trimmed to same length of spears—bite size if desired.

In a blender combine:

¾ cup corn oil
½ cup lemon juice
1½ tablespoons sugar
1 teaspoon salt

½ teaspoon tarragon and ½ teaspoon oregano
½ teaspoon freshly ground black pepper

Blend well and then add 1 clove sliced garlic. Cover the drained asparagus with this dressing. Chill at least 2 hours. Lift from dressing and serve on lettuce with slices of hard-boiled eggs.

JunE

M Y R E S I G N A T I O N is on the superintendent's desk. I will not be coming back to teach next fall. For
eighteen years the teaching of reading and language has been
a major focus of my life—not a job but a vocation. There's
something splendid about having daily work which offers a
challenge and gives a feeling that talents and abilities I didn't
even know I possessed were being drawn forth and utilized.
There's joy in being involved in worthwhile tasks where
effort and ingenuity result in a sense of achievement.

Resigning was not an impulsive decision. It was just one
of the alternatives I considered while trying for two years
to get the administration to listen and to understand what
really goes on in junior high school classes.

But let me back up a bit. The year I started teaching
seventh grade there were four other new teachers. We were
given a "new slate" pep talk and a list made out by high
school teachers of what they considered serious weaknesses
in the skills of entering freshmen—weaknesses which led to
failure and a high drop-out rate. The challenge presented to
us was to "Develop new programs to overcome these weaknesses and do everything you can to promote the importance
of learning—not just staying in school, but learning and
graduating with a firm base for the future."

We were a diverse group. Our backgrounds, our hobbies,
even our eating habits differed and this may be one reason
why we were able to argue constructively and try new approaches. Our principal supported us. The superintendent
was available for advice and encouragement. But probably
the most positive change which came out of our cooperation
over the years was knowing what was going on in each other's
classrooms and facilitating that teaching in all possible ways.
When I taught the History of the English Language, the
social studies teacher reviewed causes of migrations, the math
teacher took that week to do time lines, and the science
teacher stressed the origin of scientific terms. Everyone co-

operated in helping the students with their projects and arranged schedules in order to be an audience for student presentations. The emphasis was on learning.

Then the district built a new school and there was a concentration on things—carpets, a gym floor which had to be refinished and refinished, grass that needed planting, and ventilation fans which made so much noise no one could hear. With the move into the new facility, my class was divided into three sections, instead of the two I had taught for sixteen years. The eighth grade reading teacher was also given an extra class. In order to be able to maintain the standards and the quality of the programs we had developed, programs which worked, we asked for some clerical help. The answer was no—there was no money.

After two years of asking, explaining, begging and pleading for some support for carrying on a good junior high school program I still was unable to get any response except "Do the best you can. There just isn't any money."

It was quite apparent that there was money to pay workmen to take out and reverse the fans which had been put in backwards (sucking in rainwater to rot the new walls). No one questioned paying several referees to run around an expensive gym floor blowing whistles so five or ten students could participate in sports. The administration approved funds to plant more grass, to buy machinery and then to hire personnel to mow the new grass. Yet a request for assistance in teaching reading, language, spelling, and an improved writing program (which they said they wanted) for 120 students was ignored. Letters sent to each member of the school committee received no reponse by mail, by phone, nor in person.

So, my letter of resignation is on the superintendent's desk. Once again I have told him that I do not want to do an adequate job of teaching. I want to do a good job—to teach well. But without the support of the administration this is not possible and I do not wish to go through the motions just to receive a paycheck. Trying to teach three classes in shorter periods of time and to keep up with the planning and paperwork without some assistance has made teaching a frustration instead of a challenge and a joy. Therefore I will not be coming back next year.

For years I have awakened with fresh ideas of ways to present materials. On my fifteen mile drive to school I previewed my plans for the day and often had to stop to make notes of new possibilities to try. I've lived with invisible antennas out for illustrations and articles and facts to add to class resources. How did Tom Sawyer celebrate Christmas? What TV ads are using mythological references? There are few professions or work situations that offer the rewards of teaching—the personal rewards from student responses. I will miss the vitality of twelve and thirteen-year-old human beings. But moving away from the feeling that as a teacher I am—to the administration—less important than a lost basketball or an order of paper towels, is necessary for my soul.

J U N E is the beginning of summer and beginnings are a challenge. What will this season bring? Already the abundant green growth has changed the landscape. Shrubs in full leaf obscure the paths into the woods. Daisies unfolding their white petals look like trails of froth along the road and down across the fields.

The fireflies began their evening ballet early this year emerging from the sun-warmed earth to flash their mating signals above the meadows. Just as frogs emit sounds which attract only their kind, so fireflies blink in codes which bring lighted responses from the non-flying females of their species waiting on the tips of grasses. Night breezes sometimes delay the lightning bugs' courtship by blowing the aerial flashing males off course—sometimes sweeping dozens of them up into the tree tops. But the small glowing beetles persist through the warm June evenings until their mating is accomplished and the earth-bound females can lay glowing eggs—one by one—under the grass stems. After several weeks the eggs hatch into tiny glowworms, burrow into the earth, and another cycle begins to bring forth the bright night dancers for another season.

The mayflies, which also have but a brief span of life in the beauty of June, come to rest on my white terry robe while I'm swimming. They hold their transparent wings vertically and undulate their slender, elongated abdomen and feathery tail appendages. By slipping a finger under their front legs, I can coax them to perch upon me and observe their delicate structure. Most of these insects live three years under water before being able to float to the surface, shed their skin, and transform into the slender winged creatures ready to fly about seeking a mate.

Because these mayflies mate in flight, lay their eggs in the water, and then die, the surface of the pond is sometimes covered with thousands of them. When this happens the fish feed in schools, roiling the water, often leaping one after another until the cove looks like a stage with a fantasy ballet being performed. This is best viewed while in the pond so one's eyes are at the level of the water's surface and the silvery scales of the flipping fishes reflect the sun. Best of all is watching the feast upon mayflies against the setting sun or the light of the full moon.

In the kitchen garden ants are burrowing under my newly planted strawberries but I've discovered a yellow-shafted flicker having himself one of his favorite lunches—ants. If only he will spread the word among the other red-naped woodpeckers so they will come to lunch and I can avoid the use of any poisons. Fat as a quail, tail tilted in the hilltop breeze, this brown-flecked flicker is a welcome guest in my garden.

There's a forest of self-seeded angelica along the north side of the garage producing its huge green blossoms which, in turn, will produce the seeds the goldfinches enjoy feasting upon. This aromatic herb germinates best when the ripe seeds are planted soon after they have matured. Because it has a lush, tropical appearance, grows higher than seven feet in good soil, and has blossoms the size of cauliflowers, I've often thought of starting a "What is that plant?" situation. By rolling the ripe seeds in wet soil and then in clay to form balls, angelica might be "planted" in odd spots about the county just by tossing these seed balls from the car on a rainy summer's day.

With the beginning of this summer—having enjoyed three "resignment" parties—I'm facing the challenge of new personal beginnings. Through my orange mailbox I've been receiving offers of jobs and of diverse writing assignments and some welcome checks for manuscripts accepted for publication.

The summer solstice with the long hours of daylight and the burgeoning growth of every green plant is a splendid time for facing the challenges of new beginnings. While I'm swimming I can plan the murder mystery I've wanted to write. As I weed I can let my mind sort out columns for a book on country living. Here on Sennebec Hill I have space and privacy and this summer I'll have time—and the challenge to use it for personal growth.

THE ANALOGY between teaching and gardening crops up each year as I'm sorting, filing and packing in my classroom. Minds and soils are infinitely capacious if they're cultivated, nourished and kept reasonably free of weeds and predators.

Each June in the past I have made a September list headed by "Why not try—" and find it's similar to my October gardening journal's notes on how to improve quality and production in the next growing season. No garden is ever finished. There are always things which could, or should, or might be done. And fortunately the ability to learn and grow and change is never finished—or doesn't have to be.

This year, while the newspapers continue to print responses to the National Commission on Excellence in Education report, my annual comparisons of growth in the classroom and growth in my kitchen garden influence my perspective. Yes, there is mediocrity. Lots of it. Too much of it. And there are no simple, blanket answers which will foster excellence from Arizona to Aroostook.

Gardeners must start with the soil they have and teachers with the students assigned to the classroom. In both cases the first step is to do some analyzing, find out what base is there for growth, and then begin to add what is needed. Hauling in manure and compost will stir the microorganisms into activity in the soil, and lime will begin to overcome the acidity. Less tangible, but just as necessary, encouragement and praise usually stir responses among the students, and patience can become a neutralizer.

The weather is unpredictable. Hot sun may dry up my seedlings or cold rains may kill them off. Wind squalls break over my pepper plants. In gardening I learn to anticipate influences beyond my control and adapt to the results without allowing myself to be discouraged or overwhelmed. Flu epidemics, schedule changes, lack of supplies and negative attitudes brought in from home are also beyond my control.

Disruptive and discouraging, they must be accepted and then overcome when possible.

Spindly plants can often be revived with a dose of manure tea, but an invasion of hungry cutworms just wipes out all chance of growth. Likewise on the days when we're all set to start a new project and suddenly four students are called out for physicals, three take off for band, and two depart to have their braces tightened, planned growth is wiped out. By referring to such happenings as "Cutworm Days" and substituting another activity, I adapt as I do in the garden.

Knowing growth limitations and germination times is important in gardening. Carrots often take a full three weeks to poke tiny green spears through the soil, and parsley can be perverse in just sitting dormant until it's ready to sprout. Sometimes I silently refer to some students as "parsleys" and am finally rewarded by a sudden sprouting of response and comprehension. Some kids are like spinach—early lush growth which wilts with the first heat. Others are like New Zealand spinach—hard seeds, reluctant to sprout but then resisting heat and space and frequent prunings, just burgeoning in all directions in the joy of growing.

Overcoming resistance to growth in the garden involves getting rid of rocks and weed roots, enriching the humus quantities in the soil, regular cultivation and frequent watering. This analogy fits into classroom learning. Getting rid of materials or even furniture which impedes movement of mind or body, adding more than is required so—like plant roots—students can reach out and select what they need or what stimulates them, and varying the daily pattern, help overcome resistance to thinking.

Some people plant empty cans in their garden to attract electrical energy and promote growth. Laughter does this in school. I'm convinced that humor opens more connections in the brain than any other single strategy. When my students bring in cartoons which depend (for understanding the punch line) upon something we've been studying, I feel we've made progress.

Prevention—planning ahead and watching for first symptoms—is the best way to deal with pests in the garden. A dusting of wood ashes while seedlings are damp with morning dew will often thwart the flea beetles. Being prepared is the best pest control within a classroom. I suspect spitballs were invented very shortly after the Egyptians first perfected their papyrus paper.

In gardening and in teaching the resulting growth is in proportion to the effort and materials put into it. My personal theory is that those who hate to garden probably raise bitter carrots and mealy melons and those who do not enjoy teaching should never be allowed to embitter the lives of students.

There are no simple answers to overcoming mediocrity in the schoolrooms. More hours, more money, more homework have been suggested. How much would those remedies improve your garden?

In gardening and in teaching it is necessary to start with what is there. It's most important to have a definite, realistic idea of what you want to produce. Don't expect to grow prize cauliflower in a gravel pit nor let any classroom feel like such a setting for growth.

A M E R I C A N S have been celebrating Father's Day on the third Sunday in June since 1924. The popularity of Mother's Day (proclaimed in 1914) and the support of commercial enterprises facilitated the acceptance of this paternal celebration. But it's nice to know that it was started to honor a widower who raised his motherless children by himself. When one of William J. Smart's daughters began her campaign for a Father's Day in Spokane, Washington, she found strong support among newspapermen and the clergy. Today media messages remind us in mid-June to pause and pay tribute to our fathers.

When my father was nineteen he was told he might live two more years. His asthmatic condition—a health problem which had shortened the life of his father and grandfather—had been aggravated when, as an active, curious youngster, he had fallen head first into the flour barrel.

Mother, with red-headed determination, contacted a former teacher and found employment for both of them in the Adirondack Mountains where irritating pollens were (and still are) less prevalent.

Facing and accepting the tenuous quality of life before he was twenty-one no doubt helped to shape my father's attitude toward living one day at a time and finding pleasure in his daily observations. It may have added to his patience and persistence.

I remember the first time he let me watch him coax a chipmunk to climb up and nibble the peanuts tucked into his hat band. This project had been started earlier by feeding the little chatterers who watched him build rustic seats along the paths of summer cottages where he worked as caretaker. With a string tied to a peanut he had drawn them closer and closer—sitting with absolute stillness. He coaxed them to the cuff of his trousers, up to his pockets, his shoulder and finally to walking around the brim of his hat pulling out the peanuts and sitting there to feast.

Years later, returning to the mountains for a visit, I witnessed more tangible evidence of my father's patience. Everywhere we went I heard my father greeted with loud calls of "Hi Jasper" and "See you later, Jasper." His explanation—presented with a note of pride—was that he had gotten a bit fed up with listening to complaints about the terrible actions of the village young folks.

He had met every complaint with the question, "What does this town offer for constructive recreational facilities for those young people?" and then, "Now, if they could organize some bowling teams—"

So he waged a quiet, continuous, unrelenting, one-man campaign to persuade the adults to vote permission for the young folks to use the Masonic bowling alley. It was a long, wearing battle, and my father's victory was bound up with a charge that he was to keep order and clean up after "those darn crazy kids."

This responsibility wasn't difficult, but it did take time. Father gave his time and the village youth gave him a new name. "Mr." Carman was too dignified. "Earl" was too familiar. "Jasper" was their special title—given with respect and affection.

Father wasn't much on lecturing. He found other ways to teach. One evening he interrupted me in an exaggerated tale about a mean, crotchety businessman and with a stern look asked a simple question, "Crotchety or lonely?" then he said, "Come." We drove up the back street and parked before a big, dark house. Father looked at his watch and we waited—in silence.

After what seemed like hours, I saw the old man coming through the shortcut from the center of town. Old? He must have been all of fifty-four. I knew his wife had died that winter and that his only child was off at college. Shoulders hunched and head bent, he plodded wearily around to the front steps, up to the wide veranda, and my father and I listened to his slow footsteps sounding on the boards as he crossed to the kitchen door. One light went on. One light in a large and empty house.

Father's practical jokes are retold at every family gathering, and we usually recall that he could also take a joke when we think of the day he put the pickled beets on the ceiling. I think it was my older brother's idea and we did have mother's permission. We sewed father's silverware to the white tablecloth on April Fool's Day and waited. Mother put on the pitcher of milk, bread and butter, the juicy spiced beets and finally father came home to eat. Something was wrong at work. He was worried and in haste and while we watched—bursting with anticipation—father grabbed his knife and fork, both at once and with a quick lift—.

Father's two years stretched into sixty-eight, and although he was never in good health physically, he gave his children some healthy attitudes toward living. I'm glad I took the time before his last Father's Day to write and thank him for teaching me and setting an example "—to pay all debts even if it's only a bit at a time and to give a good day's work and just a little bit more for every day's pay and thus to be able to live comfortably within yourself."

WATERING THE GARDEN while watching the sunrise would be more pleasant if the mosquitoes were not early risers. It's also irritating to watch the birds breakfasting upon my ripening strawberries. But the colors in the eastern sky change from rose to shrimp, and the pond, reflecting the surrounding trees, is dark and green. One boat drifts across the smoothness cutting a wedge of ripples.

The onions survived the transplanting and the hot sunny days. Dry weather—not getting enough moisture while growing—can change the flavor of onions and make them strong and hot. For mild, well-flavored onions the soil also needs to be well supplied with humus, and this vegetable depends upon day length to produce single, full, solid bulbs.

The peas, which sat under water during much of May, will not be ready for the 4th of July but they're climbing valiantly up the plastic net, blossoming as they stretch. The lazy thunbergia is just starting to climb the poles at the end of the peas and may not bloom before Labor Day.

Early morning watering gives me time each day to look over the garden and wonder what I might try next. The years of tilling and adding compost and old manure have given the soil a pleasant tilth. They have also changed the contour of this hill top. The steep slope is now a gentle one and the dip in the center has almost disappeared.

Sometimes I think I'd like to hire a few bulldozers to come in and push away problem patches, level out or slope the ditches and steep spots and get everything even and tidy all at once. Having acres which could be kept in order by either a lawn mower or a tractor mower sounds neat and desirable.

The steep hill between the farmhouse and the pond provides a sense of privacy along the shore. From the picnic area I can't see the house and it affords a feeling of being away from chores—of being in another world. The oaks along the shore have grown so high and full that even swimming far out in the cove I feel free from the house. I really wouldn't want this changed.

But the invasion of locust trees must be dealt with. The three great parent trees which towered over the farmhouse when I moved here thirty-four years ago are scattering their blossoms across the lawn this week. When the bees are working in these trees the hum is cheerful and soothing. The shade is welcome on summer afternoons. But something stirred the roots and set these locust trees to producing offspring—thorny, nasty bushes which now cover the whole slope so it's not even possible to see the pond.

Cutting stimulates more growth. The roots reach out in all directions and send up sprouts which almost overnight become a new jungle. Drastic measures are needed. In spite of the industries' claims about the safety of their spray products, thinking about using such potent poisons on my land disturbs me. Ten years from now new research may prove that such sprays react with soil minerals and pollute underground water. I'll try hiring some bush-hog work first— if they can maneuver on this hillside.

As the rising sun forms rainbows in the water spraying across the garden, I find myself trying to remember past summer gardens and some of my first experiments in growing vegetables. My new strawberry bed flourishes in the space once occupied by heavy rooted weeds growing higher than my head. It took two years of covering this space with magazines and cardboard covered with hay to conquer the mess and be able to turn the soil. Then it was necessary to haul in sand to lighten the heavy clay.

Eggplant flourished there. Cucumbers produced abundantly. I built my first bean tent there and surrounded it with orange calendulas. Another year I constructed a raised carrot bed by adding more sand, lots of compost, and wood ashes and produced smooth orange roots which could be pulled instead of needing to be dug. Now this corner is nourishing strawberries. And these in turn are now nourishing the birds.

My last watering chore is filling the trench inside the circle of tomato plants. The theory behind this "wheel" design is that five super-fed plants—enclosed in strong wire cages—will produce as many full, large tomatoes as could be harvested from twenty conventionally planted seedlings. The hub of the wheel is a pit as large as a bushel basket. This is dug in May and filled with the first nitrogen rich grass clippings, manure, fish meal, and compost. Circling this hub is an eight inch deep trench lined with old manure. On the outside of this trench, five tomato plants are set into holes in which grass clippings, chopped leaves, and compost were decomposing and warming the soil. The cages, made of concrete reinforcing wire, are each anchored by double four foot stakes because otherwise the weight of the super-producing plants would tip them over. Marigolds planted between each wire cage bloom in bright profusion making the tomato wheel a glowing circle.

Dawn in the garden is a peaceful way to start the day—a time for drifting thoughts and memories. And while the trench fills with water, I feast upon the strawberries before the birds consume them all.

THE FIRST STRAWBERRIES from my first strawberry patch are delicious. There's no substitute for the quality and flavor of a sun-warmed, just-picked strawberry.

Now I'm reading about how to grow these plants and no longer wonder why many gardeners never attempt to set in a half-dozen roots. The books make the whole process sound too complicated to be worth the effort.

"Set plants into well-prepared soil in April or early May." Mine were planted on July 10th last year. "Cool weather and adequate moisture are necessary." During the hot, dry days of July my plants were protected by sawhorses and boards covered with old bedspreads which were anchored by chunks of fire wood. Unaesthetic, downright hovelish—but somewhat effective. The garden hose provided moisture. My dog, Miss Badger, could not be convinced that this hodge-podge was not to be used as a dog house and my less-than-2-year-old grandson followed the dog.

"Strawberries must be mulched for winter protection." The snows came early and my strawberry plants went naked into their winter sleep. Fortunately the snow remained all winter and the ground didn't heave them loose. With spring they stretched into luxuriant growth and are now producing.

My method is not recommended, but, in contemplating the bounty of berries beginning to ripen, I do believe planting strawberries is worth trying. The multiple instructions and warnings are written to keep gardeners from failing. Learning by doing—and enjoying the succulent harvest—should make setting another year's plants a pleasure instead of a chore.

The joy of doing—enjoying the experience, not just the end product or accomplishment—pays daily dividends. In June I rake my garden frequently. It stirs the top layer of soil and discourages weeds which are about to sprout roots. It gives a nice tidy appearance. But most of all it gives me quiet moments out-of-doors observing the daily changes in the garden and throughout the valley.

There's joy in learning, too, and gardening can be a social asset. Almost everyone who digs and grows has advice to give or questions to ask. In one morning I learned that side dressing onions (digging in fertilizer six to eight inches from the plant) before they are eight inches high will result in milder, sweeter onions; epsom salts watered in around peppers will promote more fruiting from each plant; and tromping on parsnip seeds after they are planted will assure better germination.

Until this year I had not heard the term "volunteer" for plants which seed themselves. I've now heard gardeners tell of nourishing volunteer tomatoes and timing them to see if they produce ripe tomatoes before the coddled seedlings started in the house. The basic premise is that any tomato seed which weathered the Maine winter and had vitality enough to push up through the cold May soil deserves attention. And will reward the gardener.

My tomatoes were started the day the ice went out of the pond, which was April 19th this year. They went into the garden June 15th, into deep holes in which grass clippings, fish meal and compost were fermenting enough to create warmth for the roots. Waiting for warmer weather made seedlings tall and spindly but now they're buried up to their top leaves. And I've found a sturdy volunteer so I can record a comparison.

There's joy in just being. Standing rib deep in the pond watching two small turtles foraging for a buggy supper, I felt movement near my knees. Looking down I found a school of perch swimming in and out around my legs. The movement of my head sent a few scudding away, but at least a dozen continued their leisurely swim, almost like a gentle dance, back and forth around me.

Psychologist Frieda Porat wrote that joy is the ability to have peak experiences about small happenings. Remembering moments of delight softens the harshness of life's more difficult days. Enduring hills surround this valley. The strawberry plants are new—bearing their first fruits and the tomatoes are just settling in to grow. All are reminders that life and growth and change are eternal and there will be more moments of delight if I'm willing to pause and look.

JULY

MY GARDEN JOURNAL has a notation, underlined for emphasis, "Don't waste weeds." Each time I dump another wheelbarrow load of fresh, green weeds upon the compost pile, I think of those words and wish I had a record of the volume of unwanted plants pitched there in just this gardening season.

The pile grows high and unsightly and then—with hot sun, watering, and a bit of stirring—shrinks almost overnight. Healthy weeds are high in protein and have enough nitrogen in them to provide for their own rotting-down without taking nutrients from surrounding soil and plants. Deep-rooted weeds bring up minerals which are not available to shallow-rooted vegetables. Some weeds are accumulators of trace elements. Vetch, for example, accumulates boron, cobalt, zinc and molybdenum. Collected, composted and then spaded into the garden, weeds feed my soil.

Weeds are sometimes described as native plants which happen to be growing where you would rather have something else flourish. But since I started working in my gardens this season I've had a feeling that there are new varieties of unwanted plants—weeds I've never seen before. Perhaps I'm just becoming more observant and curious—aware of the many ways new plants might travel to my acres.

Scatterings from my winter bird feeder and recycled seeds from the neighbors' feeders supply materials which are not native. Migrating birds contribute viable seeds in their droppings which may have been ingested in other states. New weeds could have sprouted from the horse manure hauled in last year because the grain fed to those creatures was shipped in from the Midwest. With each exchange of seedlings or bulbs, my garden gathers bits of soil from other counties. Some horticultural specialists have estimated that a 25 × 25-foot garden has at least forty pounds of weed seeds waiting for the opportunity to grow, so any additions to my soil could bring growth unfamiliar to me.

Since weeds are tougher and better fitted to the environment than vegetable crops, they're not easily discouraged. The "rule of ten" is one worth using in the home garden. Usually after the soil has been spaded or rototilled and leveled off for planting, the weed seeds will show their little green shoots in ten days. A good raking over any unplanted soil will break their first tender tap root before they're firmly entrenched. I have a small rake—like a child's tool but with a longer handle—and this will rake along my planted seedlings to loosen and kill emerging weeds.

There's another way of using the advice about not wasting weeds. Bending to hand cultivate can do wonders for the waistline. With the morning sunshine and the pleasure of watching the daily changes in each kind of vegetable, I find the exercise of scratching the soil in each raised bed far more delightful than the "one, two, three" some people join via TV. There's a catbird who comes along to jeer each day, but the other birds seem to sing encouragement.

The centerpiece on my dining table sometimes includes four or five different weeds in bloom, and to identify them I need both *Common Weeds of the United States*, a Dover publication prepared by the United States Department of Agriculture, and Dwelley's *Summer and Fall Wildflowers of New England*. This week there's fleabane, cinquefoil, musk mallow, hop clover and soapwort—names I'd never heard until I began to know my own weeds.

Beginning gardeners are often hesitant to pull out any small sprouts because they don't know how to identify the first leaves of what they've planted. Since weeds and seedlings often break through at the same time, anyone *can* make errors. Some seed packages have fairly good sketches of what the first sprouts should look like, but it's still easy to be confused unless your seeds were planted in well-marked single rows. With scatter planting in wide rows, what shows up most is probably the one planted.

Last fall when I pulled up the frost-killed marigolds, I whipped them along the garden border hoping they'd send up new marigolds this spring. So, when I found tiny seedlings in this area I tended them carefully. But these marigold-looking plants turned out to be three tomatoes and two healthy ragweeds.

Weed-covered soil is better than naked soil which can be whirled away by wind or washed away without roots to hold it. It's well to mow the weeds before they can produce seeds but while they're growing, they're manufacturing nutrients. The weeds should be plowed under, composted or just left to decompose.

Some parts of my gardens have sheep sorrel creeping in which is a definite soil indicator—calcium and lime are needed. Horse-tail, also called mare's tail, moves into poorly drained soil, which is not a problem on my hilltop.

Emerson said a weed is a plant whose virtues have not yet been discovered. Until the time of such discovery, constant attention to keeping them under control affords exercise in the sunshine, a steady supply of materials for the compost heap and the pleasure of a froth of daisies along the country roads.

THERE'S A STILLNESS, a freshness in the early morning hours which lifts me to reach beyond myself, which renews that deep sense of being a part of the growing, changing world of nature. The smooth, unrippled surface of the pond looks almost oily like a newly polished table.

When I go down to swim at dawn, I find myself walking slowly, quietly, watching, not wanting to disturb the silence. At this hour even my dog follows the path, restraining her customary racing through the underbrush and thus, being behind me, she misses the sight and scent of the small rabbits breakfasting under the oaks. As I start down the last steep slope, they vanish.

The loons glide past, coming out of Katy Cove and heading for the upper end of the pond. Aloof and regal they sail along leaving only a mild ripple in the still, smooth surface. If I keep my underwater movements gentle, sometimes I can approach close enough to count the white ribbed markings on their throats.

For thirty years two loons have been swimming in and out of this cove. Some years there have been three and one summer seven. I have never seen any except full-grown adults, but others who live on Sennebec or spend weekends here have watched loons guiding their young at the northern end of the pond where the St. Georges River flows in. If any loon eggs have hatched along this shore, some predator must have gobbled them before the babies began to swim.

Although the land along the cover is low and floods each spring, the row of oaks, planted some ninety years ago after a boundary dispute was settled, seem almost as sturdy as those marching up the hill to the road. In this marshy area the first whippoorwills announce their annual arrival and here the American bittern chants his monotonous pumping song. The cow moose which has been wandering through the valley during the past month, has been seen on this point by others—not by me.

But I keep watching. Each time I swim I scan the shore and marsh, alert for any movement or looming dark shape. This habit of surveillance rewarded me this week. A warm tawny color showed among the green shrubs and a deer—a doe—stepped out onto the cove beach, lifted her head and looked in both directions. Sensing no danger she moved toward the point and a moment later a fawn followed her. And then another. They grazed along the sand bar and then slipped into the bushes. Several minutes passed before they reappeared at the end of the point, the fawns remaining just behind the doe. Then, as silently as they had come forth, they melted into the thick underbrush and were gone.

Miss Badger, whose mother is a black Lab, routinely checks out the reeds just above the swimming cove, and the brown duck which feeds there objects. An eruption of flapping wings accompanied by loud protests in duck language leads Miss Badger on a chase. Duck flies about twenty feet and then settles down to swim. Miss Badger swims in pursuit. Sometimes the duck leads Badg halfway across the pond in this fly–swim charade, but as soon as the dog gives up and starts back toward shore, Duck swims right along behind. I hope Duck isn't trying to raise a family in those reeds because Miss Badger's ancestry has given her retriever instincts.

Some years the shore is alive with chipmunks but they're missing this summer. When my son's wedding was celebrated under the oaks along the shore, we had to ask a family friend to act as the chipmunk chaser because these friendly, striped creatures thought a September supper a fine source of free food.

Small turtles swim with me at dawn and at dusk. At first they keep ducking under hoping I'll go away but then, through curiosity or trust, swim along with me—just keeping their distance. They snap up the insects which float on the pond while the swallows swoop down to devour those flying over the water.

Coming back up the hill bearing pails of lake mulch, I stop in the garden to spread these ground up leaves and water plants around the vegetables. By this time the killdeer and robins are competing for worms. Although some of the killdeer are larger than the robins, the darting tactics of those red-breasted robbers often leaves the long-legged hunters with a tasty morsel suddenly gone. I've seen aggressive killdeer chase my dog when the nest had been threatened. Yet this summer I've yet to see one turn and fight any robin who has stolen the morning worms.

By 6:30 a.m. the noise of trucks and tractors on both sides of the pond disrupts the stillness. The field birds and the woods birds are singing their songs of praise and the hum of insects is starting along the flower borders. The stillness is gone but a message—ancient and persistent—remains from my participation in the quiet rebirth of another country day.

THERE'S A NECKLACE in the bird-bath—a shiny silver chain with bright pink stones. And now this garden accessory, which has been serving only as the dog's watering trough, is a social center for the feathered insect eaters. Whatever inhibited the birds upon this farm, making them too modest to bathe in public, has been dispelled by their curiosity. Just ten minutes after the bauble was in the bath, the goldfinches and catbirds were hopping around the rim taking turns at splashing.

Attracting birds with bits of brightness is one of those tag ends of information stored up from something heard or read— what one friend refers to as incidental trivia. Years ago two neighbors set up winter bird feeders and about a month later met and compared notes on their avian visitors. One reported flocks of birds including five cardinals. Envious and doubting the second woman drove over to observe and reported to her husband that it wasn't fair. "She's putting out five oranges every day, sliced in half and anchored on nails. That's almost a dollar a day!"

Her husband suggested mincing up the peelings from their two daily oranges and scattering those bright bits among the bird seed and then—on impulse—he tossed in a handful of marbles he had found in cleaning up his workshop. They sparkled in the winter sunshine, catching the eyes of passing birds, and the competition for numbers and variety in the feeding flocks evened out.

Brightness in offering nesting materials is another story. Birds must know instinctively that colorful yarns woven into their nests could attract predators and lessen privacy. When short lengths of string and yarn are hung on a fence to help ease the energy expended in hunting housing materials, the dull tones are carried off but the bright colors are left.

Barn swallows nesting in a garage are messy but when such droppings are regarded as the residue of hundreds of consumed mosquitoes and flies, such nests might be encouraged. A building contractor told me about delivering a garbage can lid full of wet clay from his home brook to a summer resident who wanted to watch these swallows building. I wonder if these birds would use such wet mud if vegetable colorings were added to it?

This summer the orioles have joined the goldfinches in feasting on the ripening angelica seeds. The killdeer seem to have had a population explosion and congregate in the driveway at dawn before practicing what appears to be running exercises up and down the road. By the time the trucks start rumbling past, they've left for the fields and the shore. Perhaps it's because the high level of the pond has eliminated the beach where they usually are found that they've become road runners.

The bomber bird which built a nest in the hemlock windbreak beside the garage has not been identified. Each time I start down that path this creature comes off its nest, over my head and off to the north with a fast flutter. This is similar to being startled by the sudden flight of a partridge while quietly stalking a deer. All I see is a brownish bird about the size of a robin with a white band across its tail feathers. It won't settle down to be observed, and neither my neighbors nor my bird books have helped identify it. She—since this one sits upon the nest—seems to live alone, and so far I have not been able to catch sight of her returning to the hemlock.

The shelter offered by the hemlocks and the cauliflower-size blossoms of the angelica attract birds to my gardens but probably the flowers blooming among the vegetables are the best lures. The bright colors, the nectar, and the flying insects busy pollinating, draw them in. Soon they're exploring across the mulch and under the cabbage leaves, cheerfully devouring insects and singing their thanks.

The value of birds as a continuing check on insect population probably can't be accurately estimated. Neither can their daily contributions to visual pleasure.

Curiosity has overcome modesty (or was it fear?) and I view with delight the jostling for space to bathe with a silver necklace.

"WHAT COLOR was the sugar bowl we used to use?" No one remembers. It was broken and replaced during the remodeling of the kitchen eight years ago. Together we recall in which cupboard it was kept, and the annual crisis when someone yelled, "The ants are here!" and it was dunked in the sink and dowsed with hot water. But the color, shape and texture? Forgotten.

But the fact that none of us can describe an object we used every day for many years reminds us that memory is selective. We're less apt to say, "That's not true." More apt to say, "That's not the way I remember what happened." And remembering together is a part of family gatherings.

My children all came back to the farm during the holiday weekend—together for the first time since Thanksgiving. My grandson, Jacob, who complained last November because his small cousin didn't *do* anything, enjoyed showing off for Sara Beth, who can now follow him about as an admiring audience.

We've all grown and changed, and while these changes may not be as apparent as those in the grandchildren, each reunion is a time of getting acquainted again. Roles change. Kate is my daughter, Ken's wife, Jacob's mother. She's a sister, a sister-in-law, a granddaughter, an attorney and an adult. All of us have different daily roles, but we come together as people—individuals.

Can any family survive without a sense of humor? Someone invariably recalls the time I attempted to give the children a lesson in the proper way to step into a canoe. I can still see the three of them standing on the dock, rigid, holding their breath. What is the proper response as you watch your know-it-all mother rise from the stinking mud of the polluted Ramapo River with great gobs of green algae hanging from her ears?

Remembering together reminds us of how we cling to pictures of each other which may no longer be accurate. Sara is the one who can find things. Kate is the organized one. John is a walking encyclopedia—he never forgets anything. Good ole Mom kept the cookie jar full. Yes, and Sara, the dog lover, never ate a cookie without sharing it with the dog so the rattle of the cookie jar cover brought the beast faster than a whistle.

Perhaps someday I'll go up attic and bring down the old cookie jar and run through a spell of being a baking-type grandmother, but that won't alter the fact that we're none of us the same people who lived here together years ago. And we don't want to be. With each reunion, we let go of distorted images and expectations and discover that we respect and enjoy each other as people.

Gardening is a common denominator. John is growing some of everything among a handicap of rocks and boulders and expanding a front yard border with bulbs I've never heard of. The Massachusetts woodchucks and slugs and the shade of the Concord woods are inhibiting Kate's efforts, while Sara's first Orono garden is thriving—small, but thrifty. The pleasure of growing, or digging in the earth, we share. Learning to be philosophical about the damage by bugs and varmints and grateful for each success is a lesson we're all learning from our seed planting and cultivation.

There were times while those three were growing up when I felt certain that if they survived to adulthood without killing each other they'd never want to meet again. I'm deeply grateful that with each reunion we seem to be able to understand and appreciate each other better. Old hurts and resentments surface during the remembering together, but we find we can now discuss past events and accept the fact that none of us knew all the reasons for what went on back then. Because each one of us has grown, we hear each other more clearly.

There's an old saying, "You can pick your friends, but you're stuck with your relatives." When relatives become friends, when it's possible to think of them as people and to enjoy them, family reunions are a pleasure.

Definitely it was a pleasure to have my children and grandchildren here. And just as definitely it was a pleasure to see them leave. The time of being a daily Mommy is past, and I need space and privacy and time to get on with another chapter in my life. And I hope they were saying as they drove out of sight, "We don't have to worry about Mom. She's doing all right."

SOME DAYS everything seems to go wrong. Not tragically, irrevocably wrong. Just irritatingly, consistently not right.

For more than twenty days not one drop of rain has fallen on my gardens. Several times—just two miles down the road—I've driven through showers, heavy toad-strangler downpours, but upon arriving at the farm found not one drop of moisture. Yet, at first light this morning, multitudes of mosquitoes molested me. And, in the dry dust by the eggplant, five fat slugs were cuddled together. They may have been negotiating next year's slug population or just conferring on the night's destruction plans but a dollop of salt adjourned their meeting permanently.

It's disappointing to see the hot sun stunt or dry up plants I've nourished for four months. It's aggravating to have to give up on photography plans. The peppers—red, green and yellow—were twice transplanted to assure sturdy health before being exposed to open sunlight and gradually hardened off. Then they were set into the garden to flourish into the planned pattern of colorful fruiting.

Along came a drying twister wind and shredded them to naked stalks. If I had been home, I could have dashed out to cover them with pails or pots or something but by the time I returned the damage was complete.

The sumac and locust, like jungle vines in horror movies, are taking over the acre around my asparagus. I have the feeling that if I don't keep my eye on them while I'm working there, they may suddenly engulf me and I'll never be seen again. The bulldozer I arranged for to make a clean sweep of this problem in May has not yet lumbered into sight. Despite the lack of rain the green growth continues—luxuriant, and obscenely overpowering.

Last year my peas grew seven feet high. I had to haul a stepladder along or ask picking help from taller friends. This year I planted Sugar Rae which are supposed to be five feet high. The drought has dwarfed them to three feet and the pods (most of them down where I'll have to stand on my head to pick them) just aren't filling out.

Irritating. Not devastating but frustrating. And then while I'm moaning over the dusty wilting garden, both the washer and the dryer decide to stop functioning, the wet dog climbs up on the clean bedspread, and the glass vase slips out of my hands and smashes into fragments where I'm standing in my bare feet. All this before 7 a.m.

So I go swimming. Taking two plastic pails I go down over the hill to the shore. It's like entering another world, for the house is out of sight, the great oaks shade the picnic tables, and from the cove the only buildings in sight are across the pond.

The leaves which fall into the pond in October are ground to the consistency of coffee grounds and washed up on the beach by wind and waves. Each day I rake the beach and carry this "lake mulch" up to the garden. There's something soothing in the quiet task of gathering the mulch and in thinking how many jobs are best accomplished a bit at a time instead of attempting a gargantuan effort on one hot summer day.

The still surface of the pond is covered with hay chaff from the fields which were cut yesterday and tiny insects which perished during the night. My strokes clear a path and on each side of me fish are creating rippling circles as they come up for an insect breakfast. Returning to shore I find a chipmunk exploring the pocket of my beach robe. The exercise and the quiet of the pond shore have restored my equilibrium.

As I scatter the mulch around the plants in my garden, I marvel at the strength and health the survivors exhibit. Not a single parsley seed germinated from my planting, but those nature scattered from last year's bed are cheerfully coming up among the string beans and strawberries—in soil so dry it sounds crisp as I walk upon it.

Looking down at the kitchen garden from my dining room window I'm suddenly struck by the feeling that it looks like a cemetery. Most of the plots, planned and planted for photographs, are six feet by four feet. Now that they're covered with the 'dark "lake mulch," the coffin-size patches stand out in contrast to the dry, dusty soil.

I can't do a thing about the weather. I can only cooperate with nature and hope. And accept the fact that on those days when everything seems to go wrong I need to change my pace and take a clearer look at my growing world.

YESTERDAY I took two vacations and returned "refreshed in body and in mind." The dictionary definition doesn't mention anything about two weeks with pay after July first—just a suspension of regular activities which rests and restores.

At dawn I swam with the loons. They sailed out of the cove, silently, slowly, into the mist. Heads high, not a ripple from their propelling feet, they glided to within six feet of me as I stood neck deep trying not to cause a movement in the stillness of the water. Respectfully we studied each other. Then, communicating in loon language, they circled each other, nodded in agreement, dove and were gone.

Above the mist, above the valley, the rising sun spotlighted the top of the tree-covered ridge and briefly the windows of two high houses gleamed—gold squares among the green.

At sunset I went out to the garden with a package of large hairpins and a magnifying glass. The new strawberry plants are sending out runners and, profiting from what I learned from my first bed, I want to direct this growth. The book says to allow only five runners per plant—one mother plant should not be expected to supply strength to more than five daughters. The hairpins anchor the runners in the direction I want them to grow so they won't sprawl all over each other and the prolific parents are snipped into planned parenthood.

My leisurely movements encouraged the swallows to resume their swoops over the garden swallowing their supper of flying insects. The water skiers on the pond cut a wide wake through the apricot glow mirroring the western sky while the cove loons' laughter was answered by their upper pond relatives.

With the magnifying glass I observed the insects scuttling about in the sawdust mulch—hurrying creatures so intent upon getting somewhere that they climbed over each other's backs and then turned abruptly about and bumped into each other. Monsterish-looking under the glass but with remarkably intricate designs. This small part of my garden was teeming with life. Looking up I watched the sun slip down behind the ridge and felt, for one brief magic moment, a sense of clinging to the earth as it turned away from the source of heat and light!

Attitudes toward vacations are part of individual value systems. I ask some friends, "Are you taking a vacation this year?" And others, "Where are you going on vacation?" And find some whose Puritan ethics toward work will not permit them to be kind to themselves—to get up and go forth just to enjoy.

Having a guest room, especially a guest room in Maine, is like having a magnet which draws northward former co-workers, distant cousins, and college classmates. The first Christmas on this farm brought a flood of holiday greetings with notes "We've always wanted to see Maine and maybe next summer . . ."

Considered from the cool isolation of that first country winter, the prospect of seeing old friends was warm and pleasant. By August, the appearance of an out-of-state car in the driveway sent me out the back door to see if the guest bed sheets were dry.

When the well went dry, when the 1,000-pound steer chased some guests around the field, when I served zucchini for the third meal in two days, some of the self-inviteds found less value in a free guest room. Country plumbing problems sifted out a few more. The eerie echoes of fledgling chimney swifts greeting a parent food-fetcher wasn't welcomed at dawn by those sleeping next to that chimney. Sudden, and am-plified by the air shaft, this sound has somewhat the same effect as stepping on the tails of six cats.

The New Jersey man who gets out of his car saying, "I've brought my toolbox. What needs fixing this year?" can come back for the next thirty years. Top honors are still held by the guests who pitched in to help scald, pluck, clean and freeze the twenty-three hens which smothered in panic during an electrical storm.

House guests, trying to pack experiences into one week in Maine, have usually done their homework well. Thus, they've led me to discovering places to visit within one hour's drive. Spurred to action by their delight in my territory, I now plan mini-vacations. One morning or one afternoon a week off the farm results in a full treasury of summer memories with a minimum of effort. I'm being good to myself.

A vacationing attitude—relief at taking a break in the routine of work and pleasure in diversion—usually communicates itself to others. Talking to other vacationers seems natural. With someone from Iowa I can share the sight and sound of the surf and when they ask, "Aren't you glad you came to Maine?" I can nod and smile. Have been for 32 years, 11 months and 10 days.

"WHERE ARE all the creatures?" My older grandson had expected to spend his five days on the farm discovering and observing wildlife, but what we had was rain and mosquitoes. Even tiptoing around the compost pile with a flashlight failed to locate a single toad.

Neither Slithery, the brown striped garter snake who lives in the perennial garden, nor Darkle, the darker snake who lives near the asparagus bed, made an appearance. Jacob had really hoped for a chance to find a small snake which wouldn't mind being held just for a few minutes.

We did find a leopard frog—probably the most beautiful leopard frog in Maine—down between the pea vines and the old strawberry bed. Greener than most such "meadow" frogs and with no visible white outlining the black spots on its back, this amphibian sat among the grasses (when we moved slowly) so that it was possible to admire his camouflage. When we tried to capture him for a closer look, he executed a super leap and vanished but each day we found him again in the same spot.

One nest full of barn swallows cooperated and left their mud-daubed nursery for their first flight. And then, discouraged by the pouring rain but being too full-grown to fit comfortably back in the nest, they perched and twittered above the garage door. Shortly after Jacob headed back to Massachusetts, the fledglings ventured forth to begin swallowing mosquitoes, feeding themselves.

Although I wallowed in all the best frog territories—between the pond lilies and the bog—not a green frog nor a bullfrog could be found. Perhaps because of the high water they're feeding back in the swamp. Usually in July the young frogs go plopping into the pond as we come down the path to the beach. But although the bullfrog added his deep "Jug 'O Rum" to the loons' evening pond callings (so we know some are there) not one such creature could be caught for observation.

Crickets of various sizes were caught. Jacob was far more adept at this than I was and we had both young and adult field crickets to watch. Like the daddy longlegs we studied during his last visit, Jacob and I found this common cricket "hears" with his legs. Wouldn't it be silly if people had to go around pulling up their pants legs saying, "Would you repeat that? I didn't hear you."

When it wasn't raining the fireflies put on a spectacular performance. Across the east field and all the way out through the orchard hundreds of these lightning bugs dipped and swirled as they flashed their mating signals. Jacob's mother waded into the tall grass to catch some of the waiting females so they could brighten the bedside of the four-year-old.

Worms were plentiful. Between showers Jacob helped me set in seedlings and spotted and dispensed the wireworms because they nibble into roots. Fat earthworms were carried from the compost pile to the garden to dig drainage holes and every cutworm was stomped and squished.

Looking at my familiar territory with the company of a curious, questioning grandson provided a fresh perspective. Jacob's eyes caught the movements of all the tiny creatures living in the stone wall, pollinating the flowers, and scurrying among the vegetable plots. Each time the rains or mosquitoes drove us back into the house, we reached for the reference books to find answers to our questions. What is the beetle which looks like a ladybug but isn't? Why are some crickets different in color? Are those tiny white worms good scavengers or bad root borers? How many days do the barn swallows have to feed those nests full of hungry mouths?"

The weather was miserable and the high water of the pond left no beach space. The creatures which should have been out upon these acres had taken shelter somewhere from the downpours. But by going forth between showers Jacob and

I managed to transplant the cabbages, replace the eggplants beaten flat by wind and rain, stir up the new compost pile and identify plants sprouting along the edges of last year's compost. And, because of the dampness, we found a remarkable range of fungi burgeoning overnight—another world to study and explore.

)

AUGUST

HERE ON THE FARM, being in the social swim means enjoying summer conversations in the pond. Moving back and forth through the cool, clean water is relaxing—conducive to sharing thoughts. There's a sensuous pleasure in just being in the water, in the peaceful quietness of the cove, and in the valley cupped between the wooded hills. Friends keep coming back.

They will pull in my driveway, and a few beeps on the horn invite me to join them. When I can leave my work, I do. Some friends are morning swimmers who enjoy the stillness of the pond's surface and the way it's possible to look down at underwater life while the sun is almost directly overhead. Lazy sunfish swerving in and out among the pond weeds seem only momentarily disturbed by persons passing over them.

Most swimming guests come in the afternoon, but a few give themselves the pleasure of watching the sunset and the strangely vivid depth of color among the white birches as daylight fades. When the moon is full and the loons are laughing, the water seems to have a silken texture. Voices soften to whispers as we move through the dark green water.

The topics discussed in Sennebec Pond this summer have been diverse. We discuss taxes, of course. The revaluation of land and the division of farms in this valley directly affect many of us who swim together. There's a disquieting element in the economic changes. After working for more than thirty-five years—forgoing travel and new clothes and such luxuries—in order to provide for a comfortable retirement, it's dismaying to face increasing costs.

Swimming with retired teachers and those preparing to go back to classrooms has kept the subject of education alive along the shore all summer. Whether the swimmers are vacationing from New Jersey schools or county classrooms, their conversations invariably lead into two prime areas of frustration.

"I'd like to hog-tie my superintendent and *make* him sit in my classroom for one morning," said one Jersey teacher, treading water furiously. "He has never visited a class and yet he has just changed the whole schedule, tossing my September plans down the drain. He wants me to upgrade the math scores and then informs me that half the class will be out for band or counseling."

That irritating but memorable phrase "the rising tide of mediocrity" echoed across the water many times this summer, and the second area of teacher frustration emerged repeatedly.

Students may arrive at school without their homework or their lunch money. They may forget their books, pens, and sneakers. But they bring with them every day the attitudes toward education which they have learned from their families in their homes.

Back and forth all through this sunny summer, conversations have turned to the journalistic comments on schools and education with blame for inertia, mediocrity, and poor scholastic scores being dumped upon the teachers. Few words are written about those higher paid administration people who set the school policies and do the scheduling—and re-scheduling. Maybe more dialogue for better understanding will develop from reactions to media reports.

Former students are part of the social swim on my shore. One group who came into my classroom back in '71 brought some of their significant others to swim recently. Splashing about in Sennebec, they filled me in on the changes and choices in their graduate years. Listening to their recollections of school days, I heard gratitude and praise for teachers who had demanded quality work. "But it was years later that we appreciated this," one young woman commented. "At the time, we fought it. About all we gave credit for at the time was being recognized as people instead of mass robots."

Among the summer swimmers there are always a few house guests who ask the perennial question, "But what do you do after Labor Day?"

Some of us keep swimming and socializing together while we watch the swamp maples begin the march of autumn colors. Others just picnic under the oaks and wait for the exercisers. But the leisurely discussions of summer don't end—too many topics have gained firm roots in our minds.

EACH AUGUST on this farm adds to my blueberry memories. These began that first summer when, while viewing the acres of frosty blue fruit, it suddenly became necessary to find the nearest hospital. In the delivery room the nurse cradled my 4½ pound daughter in her hands and remarked, "Blueberry Eyes—you're not big enough to bother keeping!"

The baby book warned against feeding blueberries to children under the age of two. Something about indigestible skins. But I found that rolling a few of these berries onto the highchair tray would occupy the seventeen-month-old while I fed the new one. By the next August they were both picking for themselves and readily digesting all they could stuff in.

Spring burning was a time of excitement especially if it was done at night when the wind had died down. These were neighborhood gatherings—families helping other families—and the suppers shared by the sooty crews were a social time.

There was often a social aspect to the picking also. Sometimes a dozen assorted adults and as many children enjoyed each other while filling the pails and bowls. One August day we had people from Orono, Portland, New Jersey, Iran, and Egypt getting acquainted in that field. It was a day to hold in memory—the hilltop blue with a good crop, sunshine with drifting clouds, and down below the sparkling waters of Sennebec.

Those who had never seen low-bush blueberries growing had questions and the men from the university found our field fine for illustrated answers. One, an amateur archeologist, pointed to the upper end of the pond where the Georges River flows in and told us about the Indians' annual trips to the sea. Coming down this waterway for their summer shellfish feasts, the Indians used fire to keep some land open—usually hill spots immediately visible as they paddled out into the open waters of ponds and lakes.

Since berries grow on new wood and propagate by runners under the ground, this burning meant a better crop of berries awaiting them on their next coastal journey. The first settlers also used fire to clear the land after felling the trees and where the soil was acid, blueberries flourished.

They also told us that the first canning of Maine blueberries was in 1866. The food needs of the army during the Civil War was the impetus for starting fish canneries along the coast. With this machinery all set up, but the market limited by the end of the war, the packing companies turned to the summer crops of blueberries and started a new era in Maine's agricultural economy.

As the years passed my family increased with another daughter and then a farm dog, Mrs. Kitzel, part collie and part German shepherd. We bought peanut butter in five pound pails and soon had enough pails for each person to use in berry picking.

Mrs. Kitzel raked her own. She would open her jaws, bare her teeth, and set them over a juicy clump of berries, back up and have a mouthful. She was a faithful purple-mouthed guard and with her the children could go alone to the blueberry field.

After the years of hand-picking and selling to summer folks, the children graduated to the raking crews and went off on the trucks on August mornings. They returned almost too weary to swim away the sweat and prickles. Half of their earnings went into their college accounts and the rest they spent with no questions asked.

A bundle of memories accumulated the summer I impulsively suggested to the Knox Agricultural Society trustees that they should have an exhibit of twenty-five blueberry desserts in their newly built Blueberry Hall. I got the job. My family's enthusiasm for taste testing these berry desserts diminished after the first dozen. The neighbors cooperated in tasting the next batches but by the time I was trying number forty-one my audience was more tolerant than eager.

The exhibit was a success and few of the viewers knew of the frantic night of baking and transporting borrowed crystal and milk glass serving pieces—gently—before the morning traffic. Corning Glass Works supplied blue and white casseroles, the Maine Department of Agriculture rounded up turn tables, Merry Gardens loaned hanging plants, Susa-Belle's donated doilies, and at the last moment a friend loaned me a blue dress so I could blend in with the decor.

The give-away recipe sheets went out to many states and requests for more came in for several years. Recipes were volunteered until my notebook numbered more than seventy-five. The Union Fair visitors told me about a dozen different seasonings for "plain" blueberry pie ranging from adding seven green berries or a teaspoon of vinegar for a bit of tartness to a dash of both cinnamon and nutmeg.

When the Blueberry Hall closed that night, my kids took the blueberry duff (steamed molasses pudding) and played catch with it until it fell into the river. Then they pitched in the rest of the desserts which had been breathed upon all day. They volunteered their services for the clean-up after I promised no more blueberry desserts for at least one year.

Time heals and cures—even saturated appetites. We will be eating blueberry desserts and sharing memories once again at the end of this August.

BLUEBERRY GINGERBREAD

½ cup shortening
¼ cup sugar
1 cup molasses
2 eggs
1 cup buttermilk or sour milk

1 teaspoon baking soda
½ teaspoon ginger
½ teaspoon cinnamon
2½ cups flour

Cream shortening and sugar. Add eggs, molasses and spices and beat well. Add flour and soda alternately with buttermilk or sour milk. Fold in blueberries.

Bake in a buttered and floured 11 × 6½ inch pan for about 30 minutes at 350°.

Top with whipped cream if desired.

BLUEBERRY CRUNCH

½ cup oatmeal
½ cup wheat germ
½ cup flour (white or whole wheat)
⅔ cup sugar

½ cup dry powdered milk
½ teaspoon salt
½ teaspoon cinnamon
½ cup butter
3 cups blueberries

Stir dry ingredients together until blended. Using a pastry mixer, blend in the butter. Spread half of this in a buttered baking pan. Add blueberries and then top with remainder of crumb mixture.

Bake about 45 minutes at 350°. Serve warm or cold—with or without whipped cream or ice cream.

Blueberry Coffee Bread

Into a large bowl, pour 1¼ cups warm water. Add ½ cup sugar and ¼ teaspoon ginger. Sprinkle over this 1 package of active dry yeast and let it stand for 10 minutes.

Add:

2 egg yolks

1 teaspoon salt

¼ cup corn oil

Blend well and add:

2 to 2½ cups more flour.

⅓ cup powdered milk

2 cups flour

Allow to rise until light. Turn out onto a floured board, knead to make smooth, and roll into a rectangle about 14 inches × 10 inches. Paint this with corn oil. With scissors cut in from long edges about 3 inches in a kind of "fringe-making". Leave uncut center about 4 inches wide.

Mix:

1 cup blueberries with a dash of salt, ⅓ cup sugar, ½ teaspoon cinnamon and 1 tablespoon flour. Spread this on center strip. Take the "fringed" edges—one strip from each side—and pull them across the filling, alternately down the length of the loaf. Tuck ends under. Let rise until double in bulk.

Bake 10 minutes at 400°, then 15 minutes at 350°.

For a shiny crust, beat 1 egg with 1 tablespoon of water and using a soft rag "sop" this gently over the loaf during the last 10 minutes of baking. Sprinkle granulated sugar over the egg glaze and finish baking.

Sennebec Spider Pudding

Grandma used her great iron "spider" for this blueberry dessert, but today's electric skillets will work quite as well.

Sauté 1 cup of white bread cubes (about 2-3 slices, with crusts removed) in ¼ cup butter or margarine, watching carefully. Stir to brown evenly.

Mix: ¼ cup sugar with ½ teaspoon cinnamon. Sprinkle this over the browned bread cubes in the pan and continue cooking until cubes are crisp.

Gently stir in 2 cups of fresh blueberries. Cook 2 minutes. Serve warm with whipped cream topping.

1863 TARTS

Blueberry tarts made with regular pie pastry are delicious but for a special "Down East" taste treat, try the kind of tarts Great-Grandmother made in 1863.

Simmer 3 cups of blueberries, ½ teaspoon cinnamon, ¼ teaspoon salt and 1 cup of sugar for ten minutes. Set aside to cool.

Sift together:
3 cups flour
1 teaspoon soda
Blend in:
½ cup butter
Stir in:
½ cup cold milk

2 teaspoons cream of tartar
2 tablespoons sugar
½ teaspoon salt

½ cup lard (or shortening)

Mix lightly as with biscuit dough. Roll out to ½ inch thickness.

Cut with biscuit cutter into rounds. Place on ungreased cookie sheet. Cut another round with a doughnut cutter so there will be a hole in the center. Dip this quickly into milk and place one on each of the first rounds of dough.

Bake at 425° for about 12 minutes. Spoon sweetened, cooked blueberries over these and serve hot or cold.

PENOBSCOT PASTRIES WITH BLUEBERRY FILLING

Pastries:

2 cups flour	1 cup cold butter
1/2 teaspoon salt	4 tablespoons water (about)—very cold

Cut butter into sifted flour and salt until butter bits are size of peas. Stir in cold water. Divide dough into two equal parts. On floured board roll each section into a 10 inch square. Prick surface well with fork. Place on ungreased cookie sheet.

Bake in a slow oven—300°—for 1 1/2 hours. Cut at once, with a sharp knife, into 9 squares. Cool.

Filling:

1 cup sugar	1/4 teaspoon salt
2 tablespoons cornstarch	1/2 cup water
	3 cups blueberries

Mix first 3 ingredients; blend well and add water and berries. Cook over medium heat, stirring, until thick and clear. Add 2 teaspoons lemon juice.

To serve: On each plate, place 1 pastry square. Spoon over this a generous portion of cooled filling. Cover with whipped cream and top with another pastry square. Chill until time to serve.

Blueberry Duff

2 cups flour
1 teaspoon baking powder
1/2 teaspoon soda
1/2 teaspoon salt
1 1/2 cups blueberries

1/3 cup brown sugar
1/3 cup molasses
1/3 butter
1/3 cup milk

Blend sugar, molasses, and butter. Mix in all ingredients except blueberries. Butter a mold (a 2 pound coffee can or shortening can will do) and layer batter and berries until 2/3 full.

Cover and steam on a trivet in a kettle of boiling water for 1 1/2 hours. Serve hot with foamy sauce, hard sauce, or ice cream.

A TINY TOAD, smaller than my thumbnail, immobilized himself on the shore path. Definitely a toad. His skin was dry—not smooth and shiny like that of a frog. We regarded each other silently until I bent for a closer look, and then with a few quick hops he disappeared beneath a stone. His color—blending with the dusty rust-brown earth of the path—was a camouflage which would have disguised his presence if I hadn't caught the movement.

Retracing my steps, I returned to the beach looking along the path and the water's edge for others of his kind. A toad that small must have hatched in this pond. For more than twenty years I've been hoping to be on the shore the day, the moment, those tadpoles-turned-toadlets move out from the pond to dry land.

The mating and the egg laying take place in April. From the day the long strings of toad eggs first drift along the shore until the day the toads come forth to live on land, fifty to one hundred days may elapse depending upon the weather. Usually the landing of the toads occurs in June, but observers have recorded this exodus as late as the first week in August. Those who have been fortunate enough to be on hand to witness this describe the event as a surging movement as though the mud of the pond was slowly coming up with gentle jerks, creeping toward the banks and fields.

Birds, snakes, coons—all creatures who find freshly hatched tender toads a gourmet treat—congregate and feast. In their passage from aquatic to land life, the baby toads are exposed and vulnerable. They can only escape destruction by moving, but this—multiplied as thousands emerge together—alerts the predators. Only the fact that each female lays as many as 10,000 eggs keeps toads from total extinction.

I marvel at the life force which urges these tiny toadlets up the two long hills to my kitchen garden. There are records to show that toads—like salmon—return to the same waters to breed, but little data on their choosing a summer feeding ground. But as long as there are enough insects to satisfy their never-ending search for food, these superior bug consumers settle in and remain within a limited area.

Gluttons worth cultivating—for toads will eat an almost unbelievable number of insects—these plump and patient creatures are a gardener's best ally. Economically each toad will consume more pests than expensive poisons might destroy, and leave no harmful residue on vegetables nor in the soil. Their nocturnal feeding takes thousands of cutworms out of operation, and they will even eat slugs.

Toad watching requires patience because their protective coloration helps them blend with the soil. When threatened by danger they will often flatten their bodies close to the ground as if to become part of it. Legs tucked tightly in, remaining motionless, they either escape notice or appear to be dead—not worthy of notice.

Toad watching at midnight can be pure magic. The beam of a flashlight will reveal dozens of toads, solemn stomachs on legs, sitting under the dew-damp greenness, their sticky tongues flipping out to catch their prey. In this directed light it's possible to appreciate the folklore phrases of the "jewel" in the head of a toad because their eyes are pools of beauty. The term "ugly as a toad" has been overused. Each summer night these gentle guardians of the garden patiently sit and feast, silently serving.

The administration in my school district used to believe that field trips to my farm were educational and so I would bring all my students—as many as seventy-five—out to Sennebec Hill each fall and spring. They had an agenda and a list of science specimens to collect. Toads were included. We carried a deep plastic pail so that each toad discovered as the kids walked through the blueberry field, down across the swamp, and up the back side of Barrett's Hill, could be tenderly conveyed.

Back at the farmhouse the toads were transferred to gallon-size glass jars so they could be observed, and the varieties of markings and colorations stimulated questions. Since in this part of Maine all toads belong to the *Bufo americanus* or American toad family, why did these collected creatures look so different?

Being seventh graders, their first guess was sex, and many females do have lighter color on their stomachs. Some students recalled the color of the soil where they had found their toads and noted that the swamp finds were darker than the ones captured on the hill. Age was a good guess since toads don't reach full maturity for five years. Food? Like humans, toads' appearances will change according to their diet. The students' questions brought answers from their own heads—toad motivated.

The collected creatures were set loose in my garden, and for weeks afterwards someone inquired each day about a particular toad. One year the largest one chose to settle in beside the front steps and until this hot dry summer came forth each June to sit in the gutter drain—a toad's way of drinking. With another rain I think he'll return and feast upon the bugs beside the stone wall. And again he'll demonstrate to my grandchildren why he's called a hoptoad. If we're quiet enough we may even get to watch him change his skin, which he has to do about every five days. Toad watching is a special part of country summers.

WHENEVER PEOPLE ASK how I can live in the country with all those creepy crawly things, I remember my first evening in New Orleans. As we strolled past some of the city's loveliest homes, my hostess explained that the uniformed men on the corners were not city police. They were private patrolmen hired by the residents to monitor those passing along their streets.

At that point I exclaimed "Something is crawling over my feet!"

"Just cockroaches—one of the less pleasant aspects of this city."

Under the next streetlight I looked down to see the scurrying creatures, five inches long, freely passing from one side of the street to the other over my naked toes. Those home owners could pay guards to limit the humans who strolled their boulevards but the cockroaches were beyond their control.

In the university housing where my friends lived, the roaches zapped up and down the walls. "You get used to it," they said. "You don't like it but you adjust. Never leave a jar lid loose, no snacks unguarded. Some days you're certain insects will prevail over man."

During my first months on this farm I was often certain that spiders, beetles and moths would prevail over men, women and children.

Moving to Maine meant—for me—learning to live in the country for the first time. To complicate the adjustment, that was a summer when the temperature couldn't seem to get below 90 degrees. And, just ten days after my arrival on the farm, I went rushing off to the hospital to give birth to a premature baby.

This small one had to be fed every three hours and as I held her in the silence (utter, unbelievable, deadly silence) of the country nights, I discovered spiders racing up and down the walls. Not little black, cobweb-building spiders, but great gray creatures as big as half dollars.

I can laugh about it now—seeing myself as I must have looked, cringing in the middle of the room with spiders to the left of me and spiders to the right plus a few creepy messengers carrying communications across the carpet.

The child and I survived, though we did not follow Dr. Spock's advice for relaxed feedings. Through those summer nights I held my nursing infant in one arm, and with the other wielded the long metal tube of the vacuum cleaner like a sword—sucking up every crawling creature.

Then came the black beetles—an August manifestation in old farmhouses. They dropped down from behind ceiling moldings, crept out of sealed-up fireplaces, and tumbled down the back stairs. Referred to as "dirt bugs" by the neighbors because they seem to hatch in the accumulated dust between old floorboards, they were declared harmless and temporary. But the clicks as their hard shells hit the kitchen counters and their inevitable appearance on the dining table were unpleasant.

The day a whole clan of them marched out single-file from the base of the guest room fireplace, I hauled in my trusty vacuum cleaner and sucked up fifty-six. Apparently hard-headed as well as hard-shelled—neither the vibrations of the vacuum motor nor the disappearance of their leaders disturbed their relentless march—they were easy to remove. Easy but repulsive. When these same beetles began to drop into my bed at night, country living lost some of its charm.

But for the children, bugs, insects, spiders and snakes were a never-ending source of interest. Their favorite spring sport was turning over rocks to see what might be living or hiding underneath and calling me forth to witness their discoveries.

To prevent them from acquiring my squeamishness, we used reference books to identify these small tenants on our acres. If we learned that a particular bug was harmful to crops, we apologized for the necessity but gave it a swift death and a proper burial. The good ones were praised and returned to garden or field.

Curiosity is contagious. That plus time and experience have resulted in a kind of live and let live co-existence with all the creepy crawly critters. If I tread upon a bee while barefooted, I'm not surprised at being stung. However, I was surprised and startled last week when earwigs attacked and bit me in my own lettuce plot. Swabbing with meat tenderizer mixed with water relieved the sting. A bit of comfrey eased the itching and the swelling.

But I've found nothing to alleviate the real hurt. Both reference books state clearly "Earwigs do not bite humans."

The clothes moths and buffalo bugs which had been feeding upon woolens in this house since 1810 welcomed the ones we inadvertently brought in from relatives' attics. Their joyful mating produced voracious hybrid types capable of digesting a guest's garments before they were unpacked.

This farm supports a myriad of minute creatures and the ancestors of most of them were here long before I arrived. I'm grateful for the help of the birds and the toads with their continuing aid in bug control—and for the long arm of the vacuum cleaner.

THE ABUNDANCE of August is both rewarding and frustrating. I'm overwhelmed by the bounty. What had been a tidy kitchen garden is terrain out of control as each plant surges into vigorous growth—determined to produce. The cucumbers are climbing the tomatoes. The green beans are leaning across the path to mingle with the prolific parsnips. Potato peelings from the Fourth of July salad were tucked under the mulch and they've sent up sturdy plants now ten inches high.

Gains from this growth enhance every meal. Small crisp zucchini add an avocado taste to salads. The first heads of dill can be sprinkled on buttered new potatoes. Baby beets the size of cherries add texture and color to the beet greens from one more thinning of that crop. Green beans slimmer than a pencil can be cooked with sweet young onions. Bits of this and that are just outside the kitchen door—tender and plentiful.

There's a margin of flavor, a degree of quality in vegetables from one's own garden that no farmers' market or produce department can supply. It's *real* food—the kind money can't buy. Broccoli with heads as tight as cauliflower cooked just to the bare edge of tenderness is broccoli at its peak, but in the markets—even in seed catalog pictures—these heads are past their succulent best.

Bounty brings benefits in socializing. Exchanging first produce involves garden strolling and swapping opinions on seed varieties and methods of cultivation. Although my neighboring gardeners may have planted the same week I did, their soil and sun conditions are different, and our cultivation and feeding techniques are not the same. Misting my peppers with an epsom salts solution may be why mine are ahead, but why are they eating broccoli before mine forms heads?

With all that "free" fresh food on hand, it's natural to say "stay for lunch" and shred more of the seven kinds of lettuce for another salad plate. The celery isn't ready yet, but stalks of Chinese cabbage provide crisp texture. Tender new growth of rhubarb chard provides crispness as well as color. Summer refrigerator staples include hard boiled eggs and cheese and a pot roast of beef or pork which can be readily sliced into salad slivers. Onions, chives, and parsley are in ample supply.

Then the dressings. I use buttermilk for the package mixes—twice as much buttermilk as mayonnaise—for flavor as well as fewer calories. There's the old family favorite made with one can of tomato soup, half a can of salad oil and half a can of vinegar, one minced onion, a tablespoon of sugar, two teaspoons of dry mustard and a generous grating of fresh black pepper. Combined in a quart jar and shaken well, it's a tart French-type dressing and leaves no messy dishes to wash up. For spicier tastes a bit of horseradish can be added.

The large flat soup or chowder dishes adapt well to salad meals, and with these it seems right to spoon on several kinds of dressings on opposite sides for eye appeal as well as flavor.

When the vegetables are so plentiful it's difficult to decide which to choose, dinners usually include at least three, and there's neither room nor desire for desserts. This kind of bounty keeps me and my food budget in better shape. Fresh, fiber-rich vegetables need no fancy sauces.

With the abundance of August, I suffer from ambivalence. Simple meals, less time in the kitchen, means more time to enjoy the fleeting summer days. But the problem of plenty plus my notebook full of vegetable recipes creates conflict. Some dishes—like enchiladas stuffed with chard, onions, and sausage and topped with melted cheese—can be duplicated in the winter with frozen chard, but iced broccoli soup is definitely an August recipe.

Cooking by the garden calendar provides new taste treats almost every day, and the bounty of a backyard garden makes it possible to enjoy the delicate flavor of squash only five inches long, eggplant while it's just the size of a pear, green beans the size of matchsticks—vegetables never seen in a market.

There's frustration in this abundance when there's too much to be picked or frozen at one time and beautiful vegetables go by their peak before they can be harvested. I've adjusted to slicing bloated zucchini into the compost but not to the waste of a fine, fat cauliflower past its prime. The rampant fecundity of my patch of earth keeps reminding me that life and growth require making choices. And that though I planted the seeds, the spark of life was already within them—beyond my control.

Plenty's a pleasant problem which can be partially solved by gourmet dining. Two cups of basil leaves for pesto sauce, gherkin-size cucumbers with green parsley dip, cauliflower and olive salad, sun-warmed tomatoes vine ripened—the rewards of August in my own backyard.

SEPTEMBER

BEING A PARENT for eighteen years before starting to teach seventh grade was good training. Not enough, but it helped. The first time one of my students said, "Look what I have!" I was quite prepared to find a snake six inches from my nose. And my years of rural parenting allowed me to ask politely, "Would you let me hold it?"

But raising three children in a large house on a 170-acre farm is different from being confined all day in one room with thirty or more active, restless, growing twelve and thirteen-year-olds. And now that I've been a junior high teacher for eighteen years, I meet odd looks and mutterings when this fact is mentioned in any gathering of teachers. The response would probably be the same if I said I had climbed Mount Katahdin on a pogo stick with one arm in a cast.

Some days—some weeks—I felt as though I were making such an ascent. But now that September is here and I'm not returning to the classroom, I'm looking back on the more than 1000 students who passed through Clark's class with a fund of memories which are at least 90 percent positive. Positive and rewarding.

When I find a note under my doormat which reads, "Not is *never, never, never* part of a verb," or "Never use a pronoun until you first use the antecedent," I know some former student stopped by while I was out. Mimicking the teacher is considered acceptable when you've graduated from her control. I always enjoyed bringing all the seventh-graders out to the farm in the fall and again in the spring. It was a school tradition—when you get to seventh grade, you get to go to the farm.

We hiked out through the blueberry fields, down across the swamp, and up the mountain collecting specimens for science class and viewing the effects of erosion from careless lumbering. Back to the house to pick up lunches and down to the shore for a picnic and more collecting for the specimen contest. One year the awards were certificates in elegant calligraphy entitling the winners to escape one detention, one test, or one homework assignment. Once a sudden shower made it necessary to store the collections indoors and a few creatures escaped in the living room but only the guest parents were uneasy.

Action and confusion are part of the thirteenth year. Perhaps that's one reason the students have enjoyed the Court of Mount Olympus. They get to race about pinning themselves into sheets before being commanded by Zeus to play their roles as mythological characters.

Their oral reports on the history of the English language have brought out dramatic talents—inflated surgeon's gloves floating across the room imprinted with medical terms, a mysterious man in army camouflage carrying placards with words which came into our language from World War II. For months they greeted situations with SNAFU and—being seventh grade—it often was "Situation normal, all fouled up."

Because reading skills can be taught with a multitude of different materials, one year we reviewed graph reading by using nutrition charts. Kids raced up from the cafeteria to check and count their protein intake and then call home to inform their mothers how many grams they needed for supper to make the full sixty grams each teenager needs for body and brain growth. Neighborhood parents cooperated by baking the pizzas we made to end the unit.

One year we had a question box. No signature necessary. We certainly learned about each other and learned to trust each other through those anonymous notes. "Do you think kids that get C and D are dum and stooped? They might be dum in school but be smart outside. Even do things you can't do." "No affance but why are you so ugly sometimes?" "Did you get good grades when you went to school?" and "What makes you like teaching?"

Teaching can be the most rewarding of professions. Not in the financial sense and not because there's much praise or recognition from the administration. But when real learning is taking place the atmosphere is as electric and stimulating as that before a violent thunderstorm. There's a glorious, intangible sense of joy each time even one student starts to question, to think, to react, to understand. There's a lift, a surge of joy like the first time you roll off on a two-wheel bike and you *go* and you don't tip over and the whole world is ahead!

My students challenged me, frustrated me, and delighted me. Being in a roomful of seventh-graders can feel like being in a hive of bees—a hive of uninhibited, curious, noisy, bumbling-all-over-each-other bees. They fluctuate from utter sophistication to nerd-like childishness and most of the time they appear to be deaf. And teaching seventh grade was exactly what I wanted to do during the past eighteen years.

SOME OF THE RAREST days of the year come in September and this year I'm free to enjoy them. Instead of being shut up inside a classroom, my work schedule can be shifted so my free time is in the middle of the day instead of after 4 p.m. Once again I can sit under the apple trees looking down through the valley while I quarter fruit for applesauce. I can pick pears in the heat of the noon-day sun instead of scuttling about with a flashlight after dusk.

A few weeks ago someone said to me, "It's all very well for you to sit on your hill looking at a spectacular view and writing about plants and trees and gardens, but how do you think all that sounds to people whose only view is their neighbor's garbage cans?"

I've lived in such places. One apartment in New Jersey was so rickety that the landlady, who lived upstairs, fell into our garbage can one night when the weight of the clothes she was hanging out tore the window frame loose from the building. When I complained about rats in that place, they loaned me a rat trap. I could have shaken hands with the people next door since the view from my window was their window. Nothing much seemed to go on in their flat but they were unabashed observers when my fellow workers in medical research served as my guinea pigs, willingly tasting the results of my cooking experiments.

Recently two friends from those long ago days were guests here for lunch, giving me a fresh opportunity for cooking. While we ate a casserole of garden vegetables and the hot yeast bread full of wheat germ and grated carrots, we talked about the dreams and plans we had shared before our paths diverged. At the research lab the young women used to gather in my office during lunch hour. There was chatter about men and marriage and social life but also daily exchanges of what was *really* important—what were we going to do with our personal selves so that living would continue to be an adventure.

At our reunion luncheon we discovered that we are once again at a pivotal point. Our children are grown. Acquiring *things* offers no challenge. We're back to examining how we can integrate the skills we've developed with our basic priorities for what will be a future of energetic, rewarding days.

While I was giving these two friends the tour of the gardens, the asparagus bed, the acres being rescued from the blight of locust bushes, and the swimming cove, I was reminded of the remark about less fortunate folks who don't live with my luxury of space and privacy.

Luxuries? Perhaps, but this is the result of foregoing acquisitions and travel and all unnecessary spending for more than half a lifetime. While my roommates were dashing off to vacations in Sea Island, Ga., I was depositing funds to buy land in Maine. Whenever there were choices, examining the top priorities resulted each time in putting the space, the view of the pond and valley, and the woodlands, first.

On these September days when I walk down across my fields and watch the ferns and swamp maples changing color along the shore, I'm grateful that the opportunity to enjoy solitude in such beautiful surroundings is still a top priority. How wretched it would be if, at this point in my life, I felt deprived because I'd gone without new clothes and a color TV and new furniture. How sad it would be if my energies were diverted by envy of friends who are off to Spain or shopping for a condominium in the Caribbean.

Someday I want to go to New Zealand, to Norway, and to Inca temples atop the Andes and if I seat myself before my typewriter regularly, I'll get there. And still have this hill to return to.

This month the sun rises in the east and sets in the west—

by the compass—as we pass the autumn equinox. The earth is beginning to cool off. The chirping, fiddling insects quiet their night songs but come out at noon, warming themselves by the stone walls, to sing their September tunes. And this year I can come out at noon to enjoy each rare September day. Luxury, but earned luxury.

WHEN I FORGET to set my alarm or decide to sleep over, I'm awakened by knocking—eighty pounds of cheerful dog thumping her tail against the dresser. Miss Badger likes to get out early to patrol the premises and dispose of any invading rabbits or woodchucks. This dog celebrated her birthday last week and—judging by her burps—treated herself to a wildlife lunch.

Before I let her out these autumn mornings, I turn on the yard lights to be certain no skunks are about. Only once have I found one on the porch steps—but that was enough. Only once have I looked out to see a black bear in the rhubarb patch and to witness the incredible acceleration of such a great creature in moving from a dead standstill to a forty mile per hour disappearance out across the orchard.

If there are deer grazing in the first light of dawn, I keep the dog inside until they have moved back to the swamp. One morning a neighbor rushed in to say, "Look out in your garden. There's a moose out there." But before I could get to the window, it had loped off behind the garage and had headed for the woods. Miss Badger missed the moose, also, but when she came back from her surveillance of the south field, her hackles bristled upon finding a strange scent in the vegetable garden.

My acres offer unending opportunities for nature watching. A fisher "flowing" along the stone wall, owls rushing by the kitchen windows at twilight, the swift dive of a hawk and then his equally speedy lift-off with a wriggling snake, a double rainbow at dawn—all happen here and need only a moment's pause to be seen and enjoyed.

Each time I walk across my back lawn and down the two slopes to the pond, I learn a little more about the wildflowers and weeds which have taken root on my land. The lawn ends in a tangle of weeds because that slope has not yet been graded so it can be cut with the hay field. Brown-eyed Susans and bouncing Bet struggle for space with the rugged Queen

Anne's lace, and behind them Canada goldenrod, with flower heads on just one side of the spreading branches, grow taller than my head.

There are more than one hundred varieties of goldenrod, and at least thirty can be found in New England. The downy goldenrod which grows along the path adds bright, well-shaped spikes to mixed bouquets. On this variety, the center of each tiny blossom is toast-colored.

Below the first slope the frothy ferns of the asparagus form a high green hedge as they manufacture food for the deep roots and next spring's crop of spears. Beside them the English everbearing strawberries are still providing a few red berries for an after-swim snack.

Asparagus Boulevard, the ten-foot space between the producing row and the trench for the new roots, has all of last year's school workbooks spread down the full seventy feet and covered with hay. This year, several cartons of *Reader's Digest* and piles of old posters were added to the mulch here since moving to a new school meant an extra June sorting and pitching of teaching materials. Will next May's asparagus have better flavor than it has for years with just elementary workbooks? Under the hay, the earthworms compost the paper while the roots of the field weeds are heavily discouraged.

Beyond the asparagus and the hemlock windbreak, loosestrife has seeded itself. These "swamp candles" are colorful here and in bouquets, but this plant can become a menace. Prolific in seed production and tenacious in its overlapping root structure, it can crowd out all other plants. Masses of loosestrife are glorious when in bloom, but they are a takeover plant and offer no food for wildlife.

Several varieties of asters are now in bloom along the second steeper slope, and more are beginning to blossom along the lower level of the hay field. The path ends at the grassy expanse beneath the oak trees. In May when I start walking down to swim, this picnic area is carpeted with bluets. This month, yellow rattlesnake weeds bloom here, looking like prim, refined dandelions on firm and slender stems.

While I walk down the path trying to identify the plants, Miss Badger rushes off through the fields and down into the bushes. She startles birds and chipmunks and sends the migrating ducks off in flight from their feeding spot among the reeds.

I think it was Hemingway who said that the worst poverty anyone can have is a poverty of mental interests. Learning to know the plants and wildlife which live upon my land and watching the changes through the seasons help me to understand life and time and insignificance of man. And to appreciate the wonders to be viewed in one's own backyard.

It's probably not more than 1,000 feet from my back door to the pond, but—if I shift into awareness—each walk along that path offers new experiences. So does the pond.

As summer winds down, so do the life cycles of some insects, and when they perish on the surface of the pond, the fish feast. The rippling circles overlap until it looks as though some giant was casting rocks. More fish appear and begin flipping out of the water in the feeding on this bounty.

Miss Badger and I swim quietly among the feeding fish, our eyes at water level while the pond reflects the sunset glow. Each silvery flip reinforces the pleasures of being— and being here—on my own farm.

THE APPLE TREES beyond the kitchen garden are heavy with fruit this year. Old trees, shaggy and neglected, they've been providing pie fillings for me and for former residents for more than fifty years.

When getting ready for winter included making and canning fifty quarts of applesauce, it was pleasant to take the kettles out under those trees to quarter and core the apples. The children picked and gathered. Seeds and stems were scattered in the grass. Most cookbooks recommend dipping cut fruit in salt water or diluted lemon juice to prevent discoloration, but in the interest of mass production we ignored such advice.

The arrival of the apple harvest ushered in an annual progression of autumn desserts. The "good book"—where only recipes tried and approved by the family were copied—has eighteen apple desserts beginning with a nobby cake full of chopped apples and pecans, served hot with a dollop of ice cream. German kuchen, made with yeast and stuffed with apple slices, was usually second and then an apple crisp with oatmeal, wheat germ and powdered milk.

Old-fashioned apple pudding made with pearl tapioca was always consumed, but constant references to frogs' eggs or fish eyes lessened the eating pleasure. After one young house guest labeled it "pill pudding," that dessert was served less often.

The good book recipes came from many sources. Steamed apple pudding had apparently been made and served in the Clark family since they brought their apple trees to Maine with them before 1800. This simple, hearty dessert requires three hours of steaming so it was necessary to remember to start peeling and mixing before 2 p.m. *Farm Journal*'s Virginia apple pudding could be slapped together in one buttery casserole, tossed in the oven forty minutes before dinner and forgotten. Less time. Less mess. And it could be served with the same sauce—1 egg, ⅓ cup brown sugar, ½ teaspoon vanilla and freshly grated nutmeg, all beaten to a smooth thick foam.

We ate Apple John—also called Apple Jonathan—because we had a small John in the family. Guests from Pennsylvania, enjoying this Maine molasses dessert, offered to bake their version of a shoo-fly pie with chopped apples, eggs, molasses and a spicy crumb topping. One of James Beard's newer cookbooks has a recipe for Sharlotka, a Polish apple pudding made with crumbs of black bread or pumpernickel. Thirty years ago it would have been necessary to drive more than thirty miles to buy a loaf of pumpernickel but when guests brought black bread from New Jersey, this moist pudding was baked in the farm kitchen. The recipe in the good book is labeled Crakow pudding.

Quite apart from the apple puddings and cakes were the pies. Seasoning preferences were settled by compromising on a bit of both cinnamon and nutmeg or—when the apples had too fine a flavor to alter—just a dite of salt. Brown sugar or white? Bits of salt pork or dots of butter? Apple cream pie was a farm favorite years ago but is seldom mentioned today. A cup of sour cream beaten with an egg and poured over the usual apple pie filling gave a different texture and a richer flavor.

By Labor Day each year, those old trees beyond the garden supplied apples for pies, but however tasty they might be, we looked forward to the night we'd have our first Old Orchard Pie. Four things were necesary for this annual treat:

First, there must be a day with brilliant foliage and warm sun. Then time without deadlines to leisurely explore old back roads, up across the ridges and down the shaggy meadows past long-abandoned farms. Finding different kinds of apples—at least five different kinds—and tossing the best of these into the pie basket.

When appetites had been whetted by exercise and fresh

air and the prospect of hot apple pie, we came back to the farm kitchen, turned on the oven and shared the pie making. It's the blending of apple flavors which makes this pie more delicious. But no blending ever tastes quite as good as that first Old Orchard pie made just hours after clambering over stone walls and striding up bush-tangled wheel tracks seeking trees left from orchards planted by long-gone farmers.

The apples ripening red in the September sun and the recipes reviewed in the family cookbook help me to recall pleasant memories of those years when energy and appetites were high. When kitchens were cluttered with harvest. When one neighbor dumped cups of sliced apples into a buttered baking pan and poured gingerbread batter over it because there wasn't a burner free for making applesauce. In the good book it's called Wit's End gingerbread, and it's delicious with or without whipped cream.

Nobby Apple Cake

1 cup sugar	1 cup flour
3 tablespoons shortening	1 teaspoon baking soda
1 egg	$\frac{1}{2}$ teaspoon salt
$\frac{1}{2}$ teaspoon cinnamon	3 cups apples / chopped
$\frac{1}{2}$ teaspoon nutmeg	$\frac{1}{2}$ cup walnuts or pecans /
1 teaspoon vanilla	chopped

Beat together sugar, shortening, egg, and seasonings until light and fluffy. Blend in flour and soda and then apples and nuts.

Bake in a brownie pan, 8 × 8, for about 40 minutes at 350°. Serve warm with whipped cream or a dollop of vanilla ice cream.

Sennebec September Cake

1 cup sugar
1 tablespoon butter
1 egg
1/2 teaspoon nutmeg
2/3 cup flour—WHOLE WHEAT

2 teaspoons baking powder
1/2 teaspoon salt
3 cups apples / chopped
1/2 cup walnuts or pecans / chopped
1/2 cup dates / cut into bits

Blend sugar, butter, egg, and nutmeg. Mix in flour, salt, and baking powder. Fold in apples, nuts, and dates.

Bake in a brownie pan, 8 × 8, for about 40 minutes at 400°. Serve warm. Ice cream or whipped cream may be used as a topping.

IF THERE'S any truth in the adage that one year of a dog's life equals seven in humans, Miss Badger is now forty-two. Certainly old enough to be dignified and use sense gained by experience.

But my dog doesn't seem to know this. The night my TV blew up—enough excitement for one evening—Badger tangled with a skunk. Perhaps she was seriously trying to protect my garden. The black and white intruder sprayed the cucumbers and green beans as it departed. Tomato juice and vinegar will lessen the scent on a dog but who would attempt pickle making with skunky gherkins no matter how well scrubbed in such a bath?

Before the polecat aroma had fully disappeared, Miss Badger came in with a mouth full of porcupine quills. Middle-age dignity and common sense? That porcupine had been dead since last November!

Badg is a farm dog. She doesn't ride around in cars and the world beyond these acres is unknown territory. Therefore, driving an 82½ pound beast suffering from pain and confusion was not exactly easy. Since the dog couldn't swallow, she slathered all over me and the upholstery. Because she wasn't accustomed to the sight of passing cars and scents of other places, poor Badg wanted to get into my lap. Her return trip the next day was easier for both of us because Miss Badger was subdued by the lingering effects of the anesthesia.

Badger's mother was a splendid black Labrador retriever who managed to get loose while in heat. The male dogs observed at that time were a large Irish setter roaming loose and a small beagle firmly secured on a run beside the next house. One or both must have comforted the lab because she produced a litter of black puppies and one pup with amber-brown feet and a mask of the same color across her face. Peering up from the box of wriggling puppies she looked like a curious badger about to brave the world.

Within six months this odd pup had lost most of the black to shades of tan and brown until she resembled a black and tan coon hound and it was necessary to explain her name. The older she gets, the more we believe that her mother sought the company of the gentle beagle next door. Although Badger stands taller than her mother, her ears and eyes have a hound dog look.

When she was small it was amusing to watch the energetic puppy leap off the floor, turn completely around in mid-air and land yelping for the food she saw coming. But when she plays this puppy trick with all her full grown weight, hits her head on the dish, and sends sloppy dog food up to the ceiling and all over me, it isn't amusing anymore. I've learned to dodge when she charges down the hill at full speed but this has upset guests—literally and figuratively.

My grandchildren, who live in dogless homes, greet Miss Badger with unrestrained affection and she is patient and gentle with them. When they're all loving her at once, she'll ask to go out but within minutes one of them will call her back inside. Their favorite game is to hide biscuit dog bones in the living room while grandma keeps Badg in the kitchen. Released, Badger's retriever receiver goes into action and with a steady sniff, sniff, sniff she finds and gobbles while the children shriek in delight.

But when the little ones depart, the dog still wants that game so each night I play hide-the-bones with her. Both of us should be more dignified but, like the kids, I keep trying to find more difficult hiding places. Badg always wins.

I get annoyed when this large beast insists upon snoozing on the sawdust mulch in the new strawberry bed and whisking off pails of it by wagging her tail to greet me. It's irritating to find that if I've forgotten to close the doors, Miss Badger has stretched out for a nap on every guest bed leaving bits of sawdust and crumpled bedspreads as evidence.

But in spite of her undignified and puppyish behavior,

Miss Badger is totally reliable in her farm responsibilities. She has cleaned out every woodchuck and rabbit so my garden is protected. I don't need a doorbell. Badg announces every arrival and she has different tones for welcome visitors and strangers. With the sense she has acquired in her "forty-two" years, Badg knows which people may get close to me and which ones need a growl of warning. Such a dog deserves a birthday celebration—with or without dignity.

IN THE FRONT of my perennial garden—much too near the border since it hides the plants behind it—is a lavishly blossoming loosestrife. I didn't put it there. It came up in the spring along with the peonies, phlox, delphiniums, and daylilies, looking healthy and important. So I nurtured it with compost and mulch as I did the other plants. Until it burst into bloom, I didn't know its name.

For weeks I had been reading about the invasion of the "purple tide" along streams in states south of Maine and had seen fields in this state beginning to blossom with hundreds of loosestrife where only a few were seen last summer. Suddenly here I was with a cultivated purple loosestrife front and center in my dooryard garden!

My chagrin was tempered by confusion, however, when the only descriptions I could find of this plant were in the lists of recommended hardy perennials. *Lythrum salicaria* was brought to America sometime before 1860 but its invasion—its takeover of acres of lowlands—seems to have happened in the last quarter of this century.

Along the Sudbury River which flows past Wayland, Lincoln, Sudbury, and Concord in Massachusetts, loosestrife was first recorded in 1958. Today the thickly thatched roots of this aggressive perennial have choked out the native wild hay of the river meadows and all the soft-stemmed herbaceous plants which grew there for centuries. The cardinal flowers which used to bloom beside that river are no longer seen.

Is it any wonder then that I was unpleasantly surprised to find that my luxuriant plant, brilliant with magenta spikes, was a purple loosestrife?

From all that I have read, the runaway spread of *Lythrum salicaria* is due to its ability to produce as many as 250,000 seeds per plant; the fact that not only are these seeds carried and scattered by birds but that when they fall into water, they germinate, then surface and are ready to take root as seedlings; and that each fallen stem will send out new roots and shoots. Moreover—being a perennial—this year's plants will grow again and again for years to come. All this makes loosestrife seem a botanical enemy—a weed to be avoided.

Only a few miles from my farm what used to be a hayfield harvested each year is now a purple pasture. Striking, bright with hundreds upon hundreds of deep purple-pink spikes of loosestrife blossoms, this is local proof of how quickly this invading plant can take over and crowd out good grasses and other native vegetation.

From my reading in newspapers and magazines I know that loosestrife is called willow-weed, killweed, and rainbow weed in Europe but not one of my seven reference books on American weeds even mentions it.

The more I looked at my blossoming loosestrife, vase-shaped, four feet tall with multiple magenta spikes reaching up like double and triple glowing candles above the dark green foliage, the more I wondered whether I should relax and enjoy its beauty or quickly dig it out before the bees could pollinate its many individual flowers.

So, I phoned Joseph Scott, state horticulturist. My specific question was whether loosestrife was—at the present time in Maine—classified as a weed or as a hardy garden perennial. Mr. Scott said that although at out-of-state meetings he had heard talk about the invasion of *Lythrum salicaria* in wetlands in New Jersey and Massachusetts, here in Maine it is still listed as a garden plant. He told me that in his own garden a loosestrife had been adding welcome color for years and that he personally had had no problems with excess seedlings in his perennial bed or on nearby land. However,. there has been some mention of loosestrife's increase in Maine and it may become a problem here as it has in other states.

It seems that loosestrife gets rampant and turns into the "purple tide" in wet meadows and lowlands along streams while, as a part of a perennial border, it behaves quite nicely and blooms in rich magenta splendor.

The very thought of loosestrife taking root along this pond, turning the lower marsh into a sea of solid purple, crowding out the plants which now feed birds and migrating fowl, is something I don't want to think about. Yet just one bird carrying the minute seeds in mud on its feet or in its feathers could start such a conquest in this valley—from my one loosestrife or from those thousands now growing as weeds in this part of Maine.

I cut off all blossoms before they could form seeds and moved the plant to the back of the bed. I'll let it bloom one more year and enjoy the glowing spikes. But I'll be watching for seedlings. Perhaps, like Mr. Scott's loosestrife, this one will—in this setting—flourish like a prized perennial instead of a rampant weed.

OCTOBER

964
CLARK

S E X in the asparagus bed sounds like the title of a raunchy paperback. However, knowing the facts of life—this plant's life—and practicing sex discrimination in this bed can prevent springtime backaches and frustrations.

Female asparagus plants produce seeds. Male plants don't. These seeds, which turn into bright red "berries" in the fall, produce seedlings—hundreds of seedlings—which have to be dug out so they won't spread their octopus-like roots and smother the spear-producing parent plants.

If only male plants are set into an asparagus bed, there will be no seed beads in autumn and no need to waste spring hours bending and weeding out sprouting babies. In general, male plants produce fewer spears per root than those of female plants. Neither sex is dependent upon the birds and bees for those tender green shoots. A well-nourished stag line of male roots will provide the desired vegetable without the unwanted seeds and sprouting offspring.

But suppose you didn't know this when you started an asparagus bed? After waiting three years for the roots to grow into manufacturers of nutrients so you can feast upon this vegetable in May, too much time and effort has been invested to consider digging out the females. Some autumn prevention will lessen the springtime weeding in the company of black flies. As soon as the green seed balls begin to turn red, cut off every female stalk and gently remove them so the ripening seeds won't be knocked off into the bed. Leave the male ferns growing until frosts have turned them yellow. Every sunny day gives them more time to manufacture food in their roots for another season.

Family planning also pays off in the strawberry bed. No mother plant should be allowed to keep producing daughters at this season but should be firmly encouraged to give that energy to the runner plants large enough to root themselves.

Scratching in a bit of mixed soil and compost under each healthy plant on the strawberry runners helps them settle in so they can get on with forming buds for next June's berries. Every strawberry runner plant which I can space apart from others will make the picking of the fruit easier next year. Using snippers to limit each strawberry "family" during these last growing days promises larger berries. Population control for better production. It's pleasant working in the autumn sunshine digging out the determined weeds which force themselves up through the sawdust mulch. What are tiny green shoots now will take off in a burst of growth next May stealing nutrients from the strawberries.

The bees are busy but sluggish in the autumn sunshine. They don't bother me while I'm cutting out all the pale aster plants so only the deeper colors will be left to pollinate. The purple and magenta asters are the most satisfactory plants in my gardens in August and September and I wish I knew how to get the bees to exchange only the best pollen so the resulting seeds would produce similar plants next year. My plans and active control may work in dealing with sex in the asparagus bed and family planning among the strawberry mother plants, but the bees buzz on about their business following their instincts.

Milkweed also ignores my efforts at control. Those I've cut down are cheerfully multiplying by sending out more underground runner roots. These push up new shoots to gather strength from the sunshine. Breezes blow in seeds from other pastures and the gossamer parachutes find my clear mown fields just right for landing. Even the carrot tops in the garden are decorated with milkweed fluff. Some weed experts insist that milkweed really takes little away from crops because of its stalklike growth, and that its strong runner roots break up heavy soils and provide channels for rain to seep in.

The birds and the bees—fewer each day as the growing season winds down—fly around me as I finish mulching my all-male row of asparagus. They flit along the seventy foot row, planted before I learned about sex in the asparagus bed. The birds will probably gobble up any seeds I've missed and deposit them by their droppings as they perch on the stakes in my kitchen garden. But there won't be hundreds now that I'm encouraging the males to be dominant in this area.

TWENTY-SIX ROBINS gathered on the back lawn at sunset. At dawn thirty or more juncos appeared on the front lawn. Such a contrast. The robins hopped quietly about respecting each other's space and feeding rights like a group of well-bred senior citizens about to begin a southern cruise together. The slate gray juncos flitted about like junior high students on a field trip. Four of them played a diving, dodging game over and under my car with startling agility and speed.

Signs of the season, these arrivals and departures of the birds accent the transition into colder weather. Weed seeds, the red berries on the asparagus ferns, and the squash seeds on the compost pile provide food for the finch tribe. The blue jays seem willing to try any morsels other birds discover, making loud comments between bites.

In late October a certain number of field mice decide to winter in my cellar and shed and there are always a few bright or persistent ones who find their way into the kitchen. Before the traps and poison pellets control this immigration, seeing a mouse head appear out of the stove burner is just another sign of the drawing in when night temperatures drop below freezing.

This year the killing frost—what some old timers refer to as "black" frost—came in the middle of the night under the cold clear light of the hunter's moon. The chill set this old house to creaking and an icy cold permeated through every room. There was a spooky quality about the invading chill which stirred thoughts of science fiction with a frozen earth.

Thick white mist hung low over the valley at dawn and every twig and leaf was crisp with frost. The icy particles caught the beams of the rising sun, turning the fields to acres of diamonds.

By noon the spinach was a sodden black mess and even the Swiss chard drooped. Only the kale and parsnips retained their crisp greenness. The cherry and yellow plum tomatoes which had looked like bright Christmas ornaments swollen from the first light frost had burst and hung limp upon the leafless stems.

In a way it's a relief to have a definitive end to the garden season. I have no yen for year-round gardening. With the produce stored, canned or frozen, it's time for a transition to other interests.

With the drawing in as temperatures drop and daylight hours lessen, an anticipation of change brings pleasure. Company around the fireplace and savory stews from the abundance of vegetables. Yeast rolls golden with shredded carrots. Squash pie. Three new cookbooks await, and clippings from last month's magazine suggest dozens of new dishes. Pork pie (*tourtiere*)and Cornish pasties are hearty autumn foods and the hot peppers suggest a Texas chili.

Although transition and change are a known factor of life, the first icy mornings are chill reminders that winter is coming. The valley begins to hum with chain saws as the grasshoppers hurry to get the firewood cut and under cover. Jacketed figures toil at hooking in storm windows and families cooperate in lugging in the lawn furniture.

The list of last chores includes oiling the handles of the rakes and spades and trundling the wheel barrows into the cellar. When the garage is free of gardening equipment so the car can fit in beside the woodpiles, there's a feeling of being ready for winter.

The transition from swimming in the pond to exercising at the pool means missing the close-up sight of geese and ducks coming in at sunset to rest and feed along the coves. From the kitchen windows I can watch the Canadas circle down to the pond, but being in the water to see their group landing adds a touch of wonder to the whole image of all birds traveling thousands of miles each autumn. Their built-in weather indicators get them up and away before our local storms.

With the time of drawing in and enjoying the warmth of the fireside, it's also time to begin to listen for the sound of the owls. At dusk and at dawn their hoots can be heard from the woods and if I watch carefully, sometimes I see them carrying off mice from the field beyond the garden. With this first autumn leisure I'm trying to learn how to identify them by the rhythm and pitch of their calls. Another sound and sign of rural autumn.

OCTOBER would be a delightful month for woods walking if it weren't for the hunters. The mosquitoes are gone, it's cool enough for hiking, and the falling leaves provide a soft carpet as well as wider views down through the forest.

But the possibility of stopping a bullet or a spread of bird shot is too real to ignore. Even on Sundays gun carriers invade my woods claiming to be just target practicing. It is true that I've only been shot at once. A myopic stranger fired at me while I was swimming. When he heard what I said, he rose to his feet and exclaimed, "I'm sorry, I thought you were a duck." Then, either realizing he sounded like the incompetent nerd he was or becoming belatedly aware of how close he had come to making a real killing, he took off across my field to make an escape in his car.

I'm not against hunting. Game from the fields and woods of this farm have been of value every year. In the days when it was a struggle to find $15 per week for grocery shopping for the five of us—including dog food and laundry detergents—partridge and venison were particularly welcome. Rabbit stew makes a hearty dinner and hasenpfeffer with lots of onions and a bit of bitter chocolate can be a dish to anticipate.

My objections are to the many weeks of hunting seasons which provide income for the state, recreation for a small part of the population, and prevent me from safely enjoying the land I pay taxes on. Posting these acres is possible but it seldom keeps out the undesirable hunters, those who shoot to hear the gun bang and leave their cans and bottles.

One October when the children were small and it was really a problem keeping them close to the house during hunting season, I submitted a manuscript to *The American Rifleman*. Titled "It Could Happen Here" the article was mostly an expression of my frustration in trying to find activities to keep the kids inside while hunters mowed off the dahlias and shredded the tablecloth from the line with bird shot. It concluded with the suggestion that perhaps I was being an overprotective mother and should teach the kids to use guns and let the hunters beware.

I know now that I submitted that idea to the wrong market. However I received with its return a personal letter from the editor suggesting that my attitude toward hunting was perhaps too limited. I felt—and still feel—that his perspective from his Washington, D.C. office was totally blind to rural land-owners. Especially those with children accustomed to roaming about their home acres.

Posting my acres would be an inconvenience to local hunters who are on the whole considerate and careful and who care enough to teach their children the safety rules before taking them into the field and woods. It would also require my hiking through the pucker brush to nail the required notices along each property line.

One of the best pieces of writing ever turned in by one of my seventh graders was a description of deer hunting. Full of the scents and sounds of the early morning scene, the words expressed the feelings of anticipation, excitement, and the need to be responsible for the safety of each hunter.

The promise of being able to go into the woods with adults when the care and handling of a gun has been satisfactorily learned is strong motivation. Every autumn a discussion of hunting sparked a wealth of class participation. And year after year I heard the same words, "Just being out in the woods is super."

I agree. That's why I disagree with the sporting laws which give that pleasure of wandering through the fields and forests to a few while limiting woods walking for those who don't tote guns and are realistically uneasy about venturing forth where the hunters wait with loaded guns. I'd like to have an October week totally free from firearms. Free for those who enjoy scuffling through the yellow leaves to hike and explore and wander in the woods soaking in the quiet and the beauty.

Am I alone in my wish to wander safely in the October woods? Or are there others who also feel deprived and thwarted by the weeks before winter when the woodlands are off-limits, unless one is willing to risk a few stray shots?

WHEN THE MOON slipped down behind the western ridge the valley was gray and quiet. A few house lights were visible across the pond. The headlights of one car flickered along the ridge but mostly there was a sense of a still sleeping world.

Within minutes—as though it had been waiting for the great eye of the moon to depart—mist flowed down the river and up from the brook which runs through the swamp on the east. The pond vanished from sight and the orchard disappeared. Thick, deep, and heavy, the white vapor engulfed my farm until even the edge of the kitchen garden was hidden and a damp cold seeped in. I built a fire in the wood stove, snuggled into the wing chair, and watched the whiteness crowd against the windows.

When the rays of the rising sun pierced through the mist, it dissipated as quickly as it had come leaving the valley dripping, clean, and clear. Across the pond in the long light of the early sunlight, flashes of red, yellow, and orange showed among the spruce and pines from the shore to the crest of the ridge.

The colors of autumn—the brilliance of this shift in the spiral of living—stimulate a special quality of energy and enthusiasm. Some is based on nostalgia. When I received my first check from *Farm Journal* for writing, I bought a red sweater, filled my pockets with apples and went forth in October sunshine to scuffle the golden leaves and dream of becoming a writer.

At about the age of ten I begged, argued, and pleaded for permission to go mountain climbing in October and was firmly refused because of the danger from hunters. But some ingenious manufacturer came forth with a harp shaped musical (?) instrument made of wax and played like a harmonica. The tones and the colors of this were equally obnoxious but—on the theory that such sounds would alert any hunters—I was allowed to climb.

The magic of those days is a treasure neither thieves, nor moths, nor rust can steal nor destroy. The path through the woods was a golden glow. Above the tops of the trees along the ledge and rocks the huckleberry bushes clung to crevices with crimson leaves spread out above the mosses and lichens. From the open summit the valley with its chain of lakes was a glorious stretch of color too vivid, too spectacular for description with mere words. It was even hard to breathe in the midst of such glory.

My children used to say "Let's go outside and *be* in the world." Good to remember this week—not to do, or go but just to be and take time to savor October.

But lazy rides for foliage viewing can be a special delight on unfamiliar roads when you've no idea what may be over the next hill or around the curve. The rolling hills of Waldo County have miles of green fields bordered with maples dazzling in scarlet and gold. Each pond and lake is a spectacle—vibrant and surprising. Coming back almost satiated with beauty, there is a new angle of light upon your own bit of Maine. The range of colors covers the spectrum—too varied for words to do half justice in description. October needs to be experienced.

Nature's shut-off systems vary in timing and texture as well as in color. The milkweed turns brown and yellow standing straight among the limper grasses like slender tombstones pointing skyward while sending out fragile clouds of floating seeds. The rhubarb, which had a clenched fist, resilient toughness in April, has flopped down giving up in a mushy flatness.

The asparagus with its tough but feathery ferns is sturdy to the end. While the fronds turn yellow, the green seeds turn red and each plant seems to try to outdo the others in its determination to reproduce and create multiple weeding problems in the spring.

While the blueberry shrubs and woodvines turn crimson,

the potato tops crumble into weak brownness as though trying quickly to return to the soil. The beans become yellow and then brown while the kale gets deeper green, fuller, and more luxuriant.

There seems to be a last surge of energy within the plants to flower or produce—to fulfill their seasonal purpose. Along the stone wall tiny pig weeds—only four inches high—are putting forth seeds. Some yarrow, defeated weekly by the lawn mower, has given up growing tall and is in blossom at grass level. And down along the pond path two violets bloom. October energizes. It's a good feeling.

D R I V I N G B A C K from Boston generated a feel-ing of escape. Speeding cars swerving from one lane to an-other, an endless rush of vehicles pinned in between apartment buildings, factories, and fences roared and hummed in a fran-tic hurrying. What will it be like when the children of those drivers add their cars to the highways?

Many devoted Maine residents—transplanted or native— have claimed that the air smells different north of the Kittery bridge. On October weekends there's a noticeable difference in the traffic and in the color. There's a lift of pleasure in coming home to Maine.

Sennebec Hill was silent. Miss Badger barked a brief wel-come and pranced among her feeding pans, sending them skittering off the steps, but not a cricket was chirping, al-though the temperature here was almost twenty degrees warmer than Boston. During summer nights insects raise a cheerful chorus but by October the darkness is no longer punctuated by sounds of birds or small creatures in the grass.

Probably most of those drivers racing the city arteries wouldn't want to live in my farmhouse. Certainly they wouldn't find employment opportunities here. But a brief visit in Massachusetts confirms again my sense of belonging, of feeling at home on my acres.

One summer years ago a young couple stopped by the farm to deliver some gifts from friends in New Jersey. To thank them we invited them to use our guest room while exploring midcoast Maine. They were both six feet tall, healthy, hand-some young people about twenty-two. Would they like to see the hens? Not if there were spiders in the hen house. Would they like to swim? Fine.

In less than three miniutes they were back in the house. The path to the shore looked as though there might be snakes. Finally they decided they would go on to a nice safe motel. That night as I listened to the loons and whippoor-wills, the crickets and katydids, and the night bugs banging on the screens, I hoped they would enjoy their vacation. But I doubted that they'd feel comfortable anywhere beyond the sidewalks of a city.

Every country acre is a textbook waiting to be studied and for anyone with curiosity—a willingness to learn—observing can foster a lifelong sense of wonder. Man is the minority in the living community on his own land—unless it has been sprayed and doused with poisons. Getting to know one's co-inhabitants is a step toward understanding the rootbed of life on this planet.

Observing first—then using guidebooks. My field glasses are kept beside the sink. The raucous cawing of the crows alerts me to their pursuit of a hawk. The killdeer's cry shows me where to watch to see the tiny young ones march across my onion patch. That fat speckled bird? The guidebook shows it to be a yellow-shafted flicker.

A few clear plastic glasses and a magnifying glass open a new world in studying the plants and insects. This miniature world seen through the glass gives views of unknown beauty of blossoms too small to be appreciated with the naked eye. A ¼-inch of a goldenrod blossom when magnified resembles a tiny bouquet of daisies. The monkey flower blossom is a delightful orchid when seen through the glass.

In the city, in the country, on the edge of the desert there are everyday frustrations of existence. Learning to make the best of the one life we have on this earth means making choices. Thoreau wrote, "We have lived not in proportion to the number of years we have spent on the earth but in proportion as we have enjoyed them."

Having space and privacy is important to me. Country living gives me the opportunity to observe the rhythm of the seasons from the myriad greens of May through the flaming foliage of October, from the stark landscape of November to the patchwork softening of the snow and earth as spring approaches.

The winding down of this year's growing season has an autumn harvest of the garden and the mind. Neighbors and friends have added to my observations and learning. Two white puffballs are growing near my front steps—doubling in size overnight. In August one grew on the south lawn until it was larger than my head, which the reference book says is rare. Will there be three rarities right at my doorstep in one season?

The Mexican sun flowers, *Tithonia* in the seed catalogs, are bursting with orange blooms, masses of marigolds blossom around the dark green kale. The purple pods of the pole beans now hang among yellow leaves. And beyond the garden the valley slopes down to the pond with ripening reds and oranges among the pines.

Driving out of Boston I felt a frightening smallness in the mechanical rush. Here on Sennebec Hill, watching the glory and power of the natural world, my feeling of smallness is one of reverence and gratitude. Man is a minority in the life on this earth and October days are brilliant reminders to live and appreciate each hour.

T H E S M E L L of burning leaves stirs memories of warm October evenings when the main street of our mountain community was lighted with fires before each house. Neighbors strolled and chatted. Kids raced and shrieked, toasted anything toastable on sticks, and upset the clean-up by showering each other with dry leaves.

Today, although this smell triggers nostalgia, I cringe at seeing all that food for the soil being wasted by burning. Fortunately many towns now have ordinances banning the burning of leaves. Unfortunately too many bagfuls of nutrient-rich fallen foliage are hauled off to the dump. Sealed in plastic, they're buried, wasted.

Composting leaves—returning their richness to the earth— is simple. Probably the easiest method is to spread the leaves over the kitchen garden, run over them a few times with the lawn mower, and then toss on just enough manure and soil to keep them from blowing away. Freezing and thawing will help decomposition and by spring they will be ready to be tilled in.

Plastic coated wire fencing makes a neat container for composting autumn leaves. One twenty-five foot roll of this (fourteen inches high) can form a rectangle or circle in the garden ready to receive the raked-up leaves. I use stakes to shape the bin, but these aren't necessary—few winds carry off twenty-five feet of fencing. By alternating spreads of leaves with soil (which contains the micro-organisms ready to start decomposing the leaves) and some sprinklings of wood ashes and manure, autumn "wastes" can become spring plant food and soil conditioner.

Leaves alone will mat, slowing the decomposition. Top soil from the garden can be used to cover the layers of leaves. It won't be lost because in April it will be returned, richer for its winter change of scene. The roll of fencing can be put away in the spring or—if you have room enough—moved to the back of the garden to collect weeds, vegetable trimmings and thinnings. Again with sprinklings of soil and manure green stuff will break down to crumbly, chocolate cake crumb-textured compost.

Autumn leaves stuffed into eighteen-inch holes where tomatoes will be growing next season, topped with a bit of manure and then filled with soil will give the earthworms a feast. The breaking down of the organic materials will warm the soil and help your tomato plants to settle in and begin to grow.

If part of your kitchen garden needs perking up or needs a rest from over-use, trenching solves the leaf problem but does require digging. A ditch 18 inches wide and 18 inches deep (and as long as you want or need) can be filled with leaves. This works well to build up humus in thin soil and to increase the water holding capacity of land at the foot of a sloping garden.

Eggplant and pepper beds will be in prime condition next June if some of the autumn leaves are trenched into the rows where these will be transplanted. Equal parts of old manure and freshly fallen leaves mixed in bushel basket size holes will give melons and cucumbers a warm, fresh start next May. Who would haul leaves to the dump if they could picture turning them into golden melons?

And if your small yard doesn't supply enough leaves for enriching your garden? Take a ride into the countryside with a tarpaulin, a grass rake and a broom. Check where the wind has drifted the trees' bounty into knee-high heaps and in only minutes you can roll up a fine supply of soil-conditioning ingredients. In this way it's also possible to gather pine needles to mulch the strawberry bed and tamarack needles to spread over the daffodils.

Since this farm was cleared in 1810, leaves have been drifting in along the shore of the pond, breaking down and supplying food for plants. It's possible to see all the stages of this progession. Weeds take root in the damp piles of decaying leaves and when they decay, shrubs sprout. This process over the years has changed the contours of the pond boundary and is continuing to do so with this year's leaves. The wide sandy beach on the south side of Katy Cove is shrinking as bushes take root in the richness of the leaves washed down the pond.

Such richness can be put to work in every kitchen garden creating earth magic—golden leaves into lush spring green.

MESSING AROUND with perennials in autumn focuses attention toward spring and another summer. Lifting and shifting the plants which gave pleasure this year and trying to visualize how large they will be next June accent the onward, upward spiral of life and growth.

In October, traffic increases on this country road. Color viewers make the circle through the valley, up this side of the pond, across the ridge looking down upon the spectacle of flaming foliage, and back along the river to the coast. Too many moan about the "end" of the season and the dread of coming winter. Their driveway visits are depressing. Sadness clouds their vision under the glowing maples.

Fortunately there are other drop-ins who bound out of their cars asking, "Where are you planting daffodils this fall?" They stuff aster seeds into their pockets, help prune dead branches from the quince shrubs, and carry off some *Lychnis chalcedoncia* roots for bright red blossoms next fourth of July. For them fall is not an end but a part of constant change heading for another season.

My shifting of perennials is this kind of looking ahead. Because this is only my second year learning about flowering plants, which come up each spring producing the same reliable blooms, moving was necessary to overcome beginner's mistakes and the unexpected growth resulting from nurturing with compost and mulch. This year the peonies bloomed but they were so overshadowed by the burgeoning *Dictamnus albus* they couldn't be seen without wading around the day lilies. Six phlox turned out to be pink and they pushed themselves into the gift *Hemerocallis* which bloomed in warm orange with rust accents.

Each time the size or colors of some of my tenderly nourished perennials elicited a "Yuck!" instead of a sigh of pleasure, I was glad to reread Allen Lacy's "Home Ground" and Henry Mitchell's "The Essential Earthman" and take comfort in the fact that jarring results can happen to experienced gardeners. Catalog illustrations may be accurate but they can't depict how a particular plant will look against a background and neighboring blooms of any garden. Nor how ten bright blooms may be overpowering.

Notes and photos of what offended me guided my autumn rearranging. I tried to be rigorous in measurements so these same plants won't crowd their new neighbors next summer. I had lots of exercise running back to the house to check on whether the garden manuals said *never* transplant in the fall or *always* divide and replant in late September. Behind the tallest phlox I found that my dog had dug resting pits which had to be filled in. Would cedar sawdust (which they say inhibits fleas) prevent this next year?

Last year a Perennial Plant Association was organized in this country and at the first symposium, nurserymen, wholesalers, and retailers expressed opinions on raising and marketing perennials. One recurring topic was the labeling of plants—especially the retailers' need to have the common name clearly visible because that's usually what the customers come in and ask for. However, the botanical name is also necssary for finding information in gardening reference books.

Many beautiful country gardens have been maintained for years by transplanting a bit of "Aunt Sally's blue," clumps of Jill's "wash house lilies," and some of those spreading things Helen brought down from Machias. But as perennials are becoming increasingly popular, more garden centers are opening to supply the owners of the new homes along every country road. Many magazines are featuring articles on easy-to-cultivate perennials. Even if neither the customer nor the clerks know how to pronounce the botanical name, it's well to keep it handy.

Reading the garden observations and opinionated statements of Lacy and Mitchell, I find something of the comfort I found years ago reading Dr. Spock—"You're an adult.

Trust your own senses." I feel better knowing all perennial dealers aren't adept at pronouncing plant names.

It's pleasant working in the October sunshine putting my garden to rest and looking forward to growth in the spring. Will the *Eryngium amethystium*—sea holly—grow tall enough to top the new day lilies? Who was it who said, "By the time a gardener is ninety-six his garden should look the way he always hoped it would"?

NOVEMBER

WHEN I SPEAK of second sight or double vision, most people think of fortune tellers or bifocals. I keep trying to find a better term for the pleasure of being able to look at this river valley as it is now while also visualizing what it was like before any settlers came and when my acres were first cleared.

Last week I was reluctant to leave the soft warmth of Indian summer and come inside when the last light of the sunset faded. Now that so many leaves have fallen, I can sit on my back steps and once again see the lights of homes across the pond and up along the ridge. When candles and oil lamps lighted the kitchens could such gentle glow be seen from here? There were houses up there on the ridge in 1810 because that was part of the stagecoach route from Wiscasset to Belfast.

The oaks along the farm boundaries and the shore still conceal some shining windows. Their leaves, now rust and burgundy, hang on to rustle in November's winds. The 1810 deed for this land reads "Beginning at the oak stump on the shore of Sennebec . . ." so, since these acres had never been occupied before, I know oak trees were a part of the native woodland.

However, the row of oaks which mark the south line of this land were planted there in the eighteen hundreds after the settlement of a dispute over this boundary. In November, looking down from the knoll on the east, I can see the copper crowns of these trees in a straight line out to the point beyond Katy Cove.

I presume the oaks along the north boundary were planted but they may have been seedlings left to grow when they sprouted from the acorns squirrels dropped along their hideouts in the old stone wall. If all of these were left to grow, the oaks would soon move in and cover that field.

The tenaciousness of the oaks in holding their leaves through November, makes this a good season to observe how many clusters of these can be seen on my acres and along each county road. The undergrowth is limited where there are groups of oak trees because their leaves are tough and full of tannin. While earthworms cheerfully reduce maple leaves to leaf mold each season, oak leaves become thick, matted layers so that even spring wildflowers are scarce in that acid soil.

Several years ago gardeners in different parts of the country were experimenting with a mulch of oak leaves around cabbage plants believing that this inhibited the cabbage moth. I have never found documented results on that theory but I know from observations in my gardens that layers of oak leaves on the paths between rows hold up well as a sturdy mulch to inhibit weed sprouting. Saves hoeing.

When the first settlers came to this area, their prime need was some cleared land for cultivation. Lumber—timber— was abundant everywhere and the price in Boston would not pay the expenses of getting it out to the coast and sailed south. So great trees were cut out and burned. A good chopper would plan according to the slope of the land and cut half through the trees. Then he would chop through a large tree—felling it toward the others—and whole rows of trees would come crashing down; the domino effect, with a minimum of chopping and with all the bushy tops in one direction. What wasn't needed for firewood or buildings was burned to clear the land.

This farm wasn't settled until about thirty-five years after the first clearings were made in this valley. Since the owner of these acres was the son of Reuben Hills, who operated the mill, sawing boards and timbers for the growing community, I like to believe that the first growth trees on this land were not wantonly burned.

On the pond side of the road the fields have remained cleared but on the east what was pasture land fifty years ago, running from the road back to Seven Brook, is now a thick forest of softwoods. Each year the alders and pines encroach a little further into the east field.

In autumn as the leaves color and then fall, it's interesting to trace the history of the valley by the present forest covers. In the past two centuries what wasn't cleared for pasture or crops was cut for lumber, firewood, or charcoal. The lime kilns on the coast were hungry for cordwood and the hillsides of this valley were cut to feed those fires. The Georges Canal, which appeared to be a successful engineering feat in 1847, was built to carry cordwood to the kilns and to transport lumber and shingles the thirty-four miles from Searsmont to the tide water in Warren. The town of Union shipped about 600 cords of wood per year and the shipping cost then was twenty-five cents per cord.

There was great celebration on the Fourth of July, 1848 when Captain George Coombs ran his twenty-three ton steamer, *The Sennebec,* up the canal to Sennebec Pond. All along the valley families gathered to watch and cheer. But the operation of the canal was short-lived. Damage by spring freshets and winter ice pressure caused financial hardships in keeping the locks in operating order and the economic situation changed in coastal business. In 1850 the last boat went down the canal and the local investors were left with debts instead of progress.

Seeing this valley as it must have looked when all these hills were cleared, and watching the leaves of this year's growth drift down and begin to return to the soil, I am reminded again that I am just a temporary resident. The earth is the rootbed of life. In the silence of these autumn evenings looking around my valley, I think of all the time and energy and dreams that went into clearing the land which is now woodland criss-crossed by old stone walls.

I need time to think through the ideas this double vision stirs before I wonder what lights will twinkle across this valley in the next century.

TAMARACKS TURN yellow and then gold when temperatures dip below freezing on October nights. But until the brilliant leaves of birches and maples drift down and the rust and copper glory of the oaks has been thinned by wind and rain, the tawny tamaracks often stand unnoticed. Sometimes November storms strip them of their golden needles before they've had a fair viewing in the parade of autumn colors.

An out-of-state hunter asked what had killed so many spruce trees along the swamp. "All kind of golden-tan from top to bottom." When I shared this with a friend who has wood lots down the coast, he reported a similar but sadder experience with a local youth. Shortly after he had given a young man permission to cut some alders, the fellow stopped in to report that—to be helpful—he had cut down some dead spruce. Those tamaracks were being saved for barn sills.

Perhaps it's because the tamarack is the only conifer that sheds all its needles in the fall—and thus looks like a dead spruce during the winter—that many aren't familiar with this tree. Or it may be because it usually grows near swamps and bogs and isn't a part of village or city landscapes. In spring its misty green blends in with budding deciduous trees. Only in November does that tamarack really show forth glowing dusky gold before its winter rest.

Down in Rockland County, New York, along the Hudson River, this conifer is referred to as the larch. Frequently as the American larch. Long ago, when I lived in that area, we used to play a game called Larch Shaking on bright November days. First we tried to see who could shake down the most needles while we counted to thirty. Then, counting to ten, who could scoop up the biggest pile. It ended with throwing handfuls of golden needles at each other, was silly and joyful and active. So far I've found no one in Maine who—at any age—has enjoyed tamarack needles on autumn outings.

In some parts of Maine people call the tamarack the "juniper tree." The Maine Forestry Department lists it as the eastern larch. The western larch, also known as the buckskin tree, grows about forty feet higher than New England tamaracks but otherwise follows the annual pattern of glowing gold before shedding all needles for winter.

The resin-packed fibers of tamarack wood make it serviceable for fence posts. This same quality will make a small stick in a fireplace burn with a fierce crackling and a barrage of spitting sparks. Spectacular but not recommended.

Tamarack cones, less than an inch long, open in the fall to release seeds, but remain on the tree all winter. Twigs with the tiny cones are adaptable in holiday arrangements.

Until I read it recently, I had never noticed that the tamaracks in November are the same color as the leaves of the weeping willow at this season. Now, on each ride through the countryside, both seem to stand out, even along roads where I thought I was familiar with almost every tree.

When a boat builder friend dropped in for coffee and said he had just driven down from Washington County where he had been buying "hackmatack knees," I was able to see and feel and ask questions about this use of the tamarack. The Algonquin Indian term *akemantak* became hackmatack and is used as often as the name tamarack.

But the knees? The natural curve where the tree trunk branches out into the large roots provides strength where angled supports are needed in wooden boat construction. The grain of the wood goes in several ways and thus doesn't dry and split. Being able to judge which root to leave attached to the tamarack trunk and cutting and blocking it out require both skill and experience.

Tamaracks are usually stripped bare by the weight and wetness of the first snows. The fading gold needles spread a last colorful blanket beneath the trees. But in nature nothing is wasted, and these needles, slowly breaking down, will sour the soil and enable lady slippers to grow and blossom there in another season. Field mice beneath the snow will carry off the seeds from the cones and—if man doesn't interfere too much—another generation may find a supply of hackmatack knees.

COINCIDENCES add a lilt to daily living. In my newspaper column about tamaracks the question about how far back in history the use of hackmatack knees might be found brought several responses—and more questions.

A reader mentioned seeing birch knees being used in boat building operations in Canada and of hearing of the use of these strong lateral root curves for trappers' cabins where the winter snows are deep and heavy.

"Too many things were never written down. History is full of blank spaces," a boat builder told me. "Think about the span of time between the first hollowed logs and rafts and coracles to the framing of boats for trade and travel. Remember man's fear of the unknown—even sailing off the earth. With the spirit of adventure, man's creative eye probably saw usable shapes in trees and tried them. Thousands of years ago and there aren't any 'how to' manuals left around."

A clipping surfaced while I sorted books. "The female blossoms of the tamarack mature into tiny cones which produce a good seed crop at intervals of three to six years. The warm, rose-brown of new cones contrasts with the golden-green needles in spring."

At the book store I picked up Melissa Mather's new book, this time a Gothic novel. Flipping quickly to page one, I find that the lonely mansion is named Tamarack!

In 1958 when the *Saturday Evening Post* serialized Melissa Mather's first book, *Rough Road Home*, with photos of the farm and family and her Vermont hilltop, many of us newcomers to Maine could identify with her struggles. That book told—with humor—of the first years of learning to live in the country.

One winter afternoon a neighbor and I compared notes on our reading of the current installment and decided we should write and tell the author how much we were enjoying her story and how glad we were that she had written it. We were at that time huddled in our jackets drinking tea while the plumber was trying once again to restore my ailing furnace to heat-producing. The problems of old houses and events in raising children are universal, but Melissa Mather's writing was so good we felt as though we had shared her copings with broken down plumbing and lost children.

When *Farm Journal* published my article about farm and family, Melissa Mather wrote *me*. When I visited at her Vermont farm, she had been baking bread from my recipes in *Woman's Day Encyclopedia of Cookery* and I was writing up a reading unit for her second book *One Summer In Between*.

Her new book shifts between the bride who comes into the isolated brick mansion in 1819 and the young widow who inherits the house and acres in 1982. Both young women have hair the color of tamarack needles in October—sometimes described as apricot and sometimes as dusky tangerine. *Emelie* evokes sympathy for both heroines and weaves in the tales so often told of how personalities can continue to influence houses long after the dominant ones are dead.

The pattern of coincidences continues. In a book about Indians, brought down from the attic, the stitching of birch bark canoes is illustrated. The birch trees of the virgin forests were greater in girth than those we see today, so that one round of bark would reach the full width and depth of the craft. And these were stitched together with the slender, strong roots of the tamarack trees.

A reader in South Carolina says she has never seen a tamarack tree. They survive the deep cold of northern Canada but seldom are found south of Pennsylvania. Enchanting trees, tamaracks. Come spring I think I'll plant one where I can watch its spring and autumn changes.

SOMEDAY I'm going to *really* clean out my garage. I try not to think about the remarks tidy types might make while doing a total clear-out should I get trampled by a moose. Instead, I focus on making room for the car to winter under cover.

The car moves out when the swallows return to nest in the garage. Bird droppings from nest building and other natural functions ruin the exterior finish. Some of these friendly swallows have considered the interior of the car a possible nest site when the vehicle was left inside the garage with the windows rolled down. Parking in the driveway is a small price to pay for the flies and mosquitoes these beautiful birds consume and the daily aerial acrobatics they perform over the garden and the pond.

Sawhorses and old planks move into the garage in May to hold the seedlings while they harden off before planting. From then until November I practice procrastination in dealing with things by saying, "Just put it in the garage," I do. They do. Everyone does until the truth of a twisted Parkinson's Law is obvious—"stuff expands to fill space available."

The filled space provides evidence of things I plan to do someday. The long green sticks—pieces from a broken trellis—need just a few cross bars to function again. They'll stack up with the poles for next year's bean tent. Every grandchild needs a bean tent for a shady retreat. The plastic foam flotation blocks can be piled up. Next spring probably I'll build a diving float to replace the one two evil boys stole and chopped into pieces.

That one hip boot needs to come out to be scrubbed. This year I really intend to stuff it, spray paint it, and set it on the door step full of pine boughs and black alder branches— the ones with bright red berries. The pair of cowboy boots can hang up. Someone always needs mud boots for emergencies in March. They don't take much room.

Those lawn chairs with shredded webbing better go by the

shed stairs with the ones from last year and the year before. Some night I could sit before the fire, read the directions on the repair kit I bought in 1980, and mend those chairs. It's a good plan.

The four five-gallon pails which leak will fit under the sawhorses. That size pail isn't easy to come by and sawdust, pine needles, and hop toads (cushioned with damp grass) can be toted even if the pails will no longer hold water. The old tennis balls can sit in a pail. If Miss Badger wants to play dog tag in the snow, they'll be handy.

Will the bird feeders get repaired this fall? They're too good to throw away but maybe I don't need four. However, they'll fit in behind the fifty-pound bag of cacao husks. These make a neat mulch around perennials and I'm glad I have a friend whose family used to own a chocolate factory. But because I'm still shifting plants, the burlap bag is still in the garage.

The someday syndrome shows itself in the frequent use of "It might come in handy" and "surely *someone* could make use of that." Someone did carry off seven old tires, three door knobs, and a roll of chicken wire. That left room to move in the screens which need new wire mesh and should be handy in case there's time this winter. And those interesting wrought iron pieces don't take much room and do need studying.

I'd like to believe that there are phases of the moon when a mood of pitching surfaces, overcoming all the hemming and hawing and waiting for certainty. About half-way through the garage cleaning I might have leaned toward tossing half the stuff into a pick-up headed for the dump—if one had appeared. Then it became a challenge to fit the old cellar door and the boards which were about that length in between the wood pile and the car space and the cultch habit won again.

The sled can be fixed for the grandchildren. That one ski

must have a use. It's possible to buy new handles for the tools sorted out. I know. I inquired last November.

The temperature dropped the first night the car went back into the garage. In the darkness I found the path between the wheelbarrow and the woodpile wide enough to maneuver with armfuls of wood. Progress over procrastination until the swallows come back in the spring.

M O L E H I L L S began to appear along the front of my perennial border early in the fall—soon after I had improved the soil by adding old manure and compost. Each morning there would be a few volcano-shaped mounds on the edge of the driveway beside the old beams which hold back the earth of the raised bed. When these piles of earth increased in both size and number, learning more about moles seemed necessary.

Moles have always lived on this farm. The cats used to deposit them on the doorstep—proving their prowess and indicating their dislike of mole meat. I've seen the soft furred creatures nosing out of tunnels in the fields and in the woods.

A quick, casual checking on the habits of the three kinds of moles found in Maine provided the comforting information that one mole devours thirty pounds of grubs, cutworms, and insects in a year's time. Such useful creatures should be welcomed.

When friends complained in the spring that moles had eaten their tulip and daffodil bulbs, I took another look at the reference books. Field mice using moles' runways nibble on roots, bark, bulbs, and tubers but moles stick to a diet of grubs, insects, and earthworms. Earthworms? I don't want any creature eating thirty pounds of the earthworms I've nourished with rich compost and maple leaves.

Thus, since the presence of moles indicates good soil with healthy earthworms, my work in improving my perennial bed has encouraged these tunnel diggers to move in. Perhaps they will devour more grubs and wireworms than good earthworms. But, if those bright-eyed field mice also move in, my careful shifting of perennials may be destroyed.

There's a conflict. The tunnels which moles dig help the earth by letting in air and water and their constant feeding upon slugs, cutworms, and insects benefits my gardens. But their consuming the earthworms which I need to aerate and fertilize the soil and creating passageways for hungry mice is detrimental.

Biologists who have studied moles suggest that probably there aren't more than two moles per half-acre and once they've done their preliminary digging of a tunnel system, they'll just run back and forth feeding there. In other words—learn to live with your moles. Some researchers report that moles consume baby mice, so if the tunnel digger isn't frightened away, the destructive mice may not move in.

Before World War I, moleskins were valued for high fashion. The soft fur is like velvet and as many as a million moleskins were sold each year to trim collars and cuffs and to make muffs and pocket linings. Mole trapping was a profitable sideline.

Isn't there a conflict here too? If there are only about four moles living on an acre, how profitable could trapping be? Unlike mice, moles breed only once a year and each female usually produces four young. When the young moles migrate to find a territory for themselves, they are often taken as prey by predatory birds. However, if a million moles *used* to become velvety trimmings, then there must be many more moles breeding these days.

New molehills are usually found when the weather begins to get colder and indicate either where a mole is beginning a tunnel system or repairing one which has caved in from surface pressure. That's what the reference books say. Then, since garden soil was hauled in this fall to build this border, my mole must be a newcomer. Then why so many molehills? Because he or she is building a complex tunnel system with five or six exits to the driveway?

Moles are usually less than six inches long and weigh only three or four ounces. But their powerful digging paws with five toes can evacuate ten pounds of soil in less than half an hour. No wonder these paws were part of magic and folklore and that in the British Highlands old folks still carry them to ward off rheumatism.

Some powerful mole paws are at work in my garden and each morning I find new molehills. Although every source I've consulted states that moles hate each other and will not share the same territory—especially the same tunnel system—the piles or tumps being heaped up each night seem too much for one mole. Either super-mole has moved in or the succulent compost-fed earthworms are tranquilizing ancient animosities.

T H E L E A V E S which extend my old oak table are reminders of the important part this piece of furniture has played in country living. Closed, this drop leaf table measures only 2 feet by 3½ feet but, with four leaves added, a dozen people can dine together with comfortable elbow room.

Stripped of the tablecloth its seven-foot surface stirs creative projects. It's splendid for cutting and pasting wallpaper, making Christmas wreaths, laying out patterns for sewing, or organizing a bean factory to see how many quarts might be canned on one summer day.

About thirty years ago I received a phone call asking if I could use an old oak table—not beautiful but serviceable—and set forth with the farm truck to pick it up. Ida Hughes had sold her house and was negotiating with several dealers to dispose of her funiture. When one dealer offered her $2 for the kitchen table, Ida declared, "Before I would sell that table for $2, I'd give it to a good woman." My volunteer work at the elementary school where Ida was principal apparently earned for me the opportunity to accept the serviceable table.

Since Ida Hughes was born in 1899 and the table had belonged to her mother, it can be classified as an antique. When the white paint was sanded from the top, the golden oak turned out to be stained with ink. Several bottles must have spilled in those years when Ida corrected papers and wrote reports.

The extension leaves were missing. Ida had loaned them to someone years before and they had never been returned. The search for oak leaves with four pegs led us into second-hand shops and country auctions where—if the price was right—we picked up table leaves of many shapes and sizes with a plan for splendid book shelves. Eventually in an old barn we found four four-pegged leaves, a neat rack for holding them, and an iron bed with gargoyles grinning down from the rails across the head of the bed.

The table has served some function in every room. Yes, even the old bathroom when it was being papered. The summers when foreign exchange students lived with us we moved the table into the shed where it could be opened full length to seat the steady stream of guests. The summer I turned down teaching jobs and gambled on earning the same amount of money by writing, the table became a desk in my bedroom.

There were years when the disappearing tail lights of the Thanksgiving guests signaled a rattling of bowls as we used the extended table to begin mixing Christmas cookies. When college years brought a need for evening gowns, lengths of red velvet and bolts of silver-flecked white were spread over the table as soon as the holiday meal was finished. And before the Sunday departure for the university, gowns for festivities were completed and packed.

Around this old table 4-H girls learned to make yeast bread—eight could knead in harmony. *Woman's Day* published "Bowl Breads For Beginners" based on these experiences and many cooks, who had never tried making bread before, started baking loaves using these recipes.

Evergreens snipped from woodland walks were woven into wreaths and ropes upon this table. Smooth stones collected from ocean beaches were built into a creche and driftwood from Moosehead was polished and shaped as background for Christmas figures—scenes to decorate the mantel. Scissors and paste covered the table surface for completing school projects. One "art" assignment, requiring originality, incorporated colored lint collected from the washing machine filter. Shaggy turkish towels worked as a base for stringing necklaces from collections of broken beads. Designs could be tried and changed before the fish line was threaded through to hold them.

Miss Badger escapes to the shelter of the table when too many people disturb her doggy privacy and the grandchildren climb under to pat her soft ears. There's room for all of them.

Christmas gifts are wrapped upon the spacious surface and puzzles sorted to check for missing pieces.

Here we enjoy Thanksgiving as a family and then the grandchildren spread their papers and markers for drawing dragons.

As I put two leaves away and changed the table pad and tablecloth size for a smaller supper party, reminders flowed in. This old drop leaf table is probably the most practical article of funiture any country house could have.

ARE THERE other families where there's a bit of Thanksgiving Day guilt? Where the women are confessing—if only to themselves—that in past years they always cheated the men folks out of the fabled joys of this holiday gathering?

Looking back at all the family get-togethers here on the farm, I'm sure that if we women had taken an objective look at the situation some arrangements about taking turns could have been accomplished. It wasn't really necessary every year for men to be out hiking through the silent woods while we monopolized the cheerful togetherness of preparing the holiday dinner and enjoyed the noisy socializing of the houseful of small cousins.

Warmly garbed in orange jackets we women could have been generous enough to leave the men to cook and referee while we wore ourselves out tramping through the forest. Since no one in my recollections ever shot a deer on Thanksgiving Day anyhow, we could have stashed the guns in the barn as we went out and been unencumbered as we wandered through the woods.

From the vantage point of the long stone wall leading down to the swamp we could have observed the wildlife trails, watched the squirrels and partridges, and caught up on our annual talk about family life.

Returning at dusk with rosy cheeks and frozen toes, we could have plopped ourselves down before the living room fire to rest while dinner was being served. Probably—with enough forethought—we could have taken that after dinner nap while the men wiped off the assorted cousins and settled them into cribs before they tackled the dirty dishes and refrigerator juggling to get the leftovers put away.

That cheery Norman Rockwell picture of the happy Walton family was, alas, denied to the men in all the family gatherings on this farm. I often think of what they missed by being out in the woods all day.

Sometimes I think I'd like to interview some of the people

responsible for the media visions of family holidays and ask if they do truly believe in such delightful togetherness. In real life when you know that Uncle Henry hasn't spoken to Cousin Claude for ten years, it's a bit ridiculous to expect that after the Thanksgiving dinner grace those two are going to be thankful that they're seated across the table from one another. If Aunt Hattie erupts into shrill tirades each time she sees bearded young men, being thankful for a well-stuffed turkey isn't going to soften her reaction to your niece's hirsute suitor.

If I'm going to reminisce about Thanksgiving perhaps I should begin with the first one. I don't mean that one by the big rock with the weary women in their unwashed British import gowns kneeling around a smokey hearth to baste the greasy game.

I mean the first one I recall, when my older brother spoiled the whole day by getting peppered with buck shot and the dinner dried out while the doctor pried out the pellets. On that Thanksgiving day the rest of us were told to be thankful because brother Bill had deliberately disobeyed and worn father's new mouton jacket. That fleecy garment was never the same again—it shed shot for months—but after having to stand up to eat for several days, Bill went forth as a blessed survivor with all his sins forgiven.

There was the year the pumpkin pie turned upside down on its way to the oven and the chasing children hit the goop at full speed. The year we journeyed forth to join the relatives with the pies and vegetables carefully packed in the car trunk. But the lock jammed and dinner waited until someone found the tools to remove the back seat and extract the food.

Having stuffed and roasted more than 900 pounds of Thanksgiving turkeys and spent many a holiday evening singing "Nobody Knows the Dishes I've Washed," there's a perversity which persists in my Thanksgiving thinking. In spite of the repetition of media images of family gatherings which are all sugar and spice and everything nice, the folks who share this day together remain human beings. And all such creatures have their limitations even on this November Thursday.

In joining hands for the traditional grace before dinner—expressing thanks as those Pilgrims did—it's a good idea to take a quick peek at the family and friends and say a little extra thanks because the creator stuffed into us a sense of humor. When we gather together that's more important than the turkey.

DECEMBER

S O M E D A Y I'm going to have a used mouse trap sale. In the newspaper advertisement I will state that these are use-tested, effective, blood stained mouse traps. By the time I have the sale, they may even be antique mouse traps. Because I have this problem.

Every fall mice come into my house. This is normal mouse behavior and I suspect the local mice have been doing this since the first part of this farmhouse was built in 1810. For generations (and a mouse generation is about two months) mother mice have been showing their offspring the cracks in this old stone foundation and teaching them the techniques of scurrying in while the autumn harvests are being brought through open doors.

Night noises each October lead me to believe that the Sennebec Hill mice offer conducted tours through the old walls with all newcomers and guests assembling at midnight in the spaces just behind my bed. Tour guides encourage cross-rafter races under the attic floor and offer prizes to the young mice who can tip the caps off the jam jars and nibble holes in the paraffin.

By the time the snow comes and the house is snugly buttoned up, the current mouse population is established and cozily producing more generations. There are always a few dumb mouslings who tumble down the attic stairs into canning jars. Doesn't everyone have canning jars on their back stairs waiting to be carried up attic? The wee mice who miss the jars just run about squeaking and scratching because they can't get back upstairs. In either case they perish and smell.

The fall the original part of this farmhouse was remodeled—an expensive and idiotic process of removing the outside walls and replacing them—the mice of Sennebec Hill sent out mouse calls for a family reunion. It was held in October and attendance was overwhelming. All the mice loved being back in the old homestead. Nostalgia, plus basic autumnal-mouse-mindedness about winter living, prompted a good 400 to settle in.

It was at this point that my collection of mouse traps began. The daily routine became familiar:

Shut off the alarm clock and remove dead mouse from trap on dresser. Turn on light to avoid stepping in four traps on bathroom floor. Empty those. Collect all dead mice from living room, dining room, and kitchen. Re-set traps. Then make coffee.

I didn't buy fancy traps—simple old snapper type. If I ran out of cheese, a bit of peanut butter or bacon was enticing. The re-baiting wasn't exactly pleasant—especially if the blood of the last victim was still warm on the trap. But one learns to cope. It was mice or me.

By March the big invasion had been stemmed and the blood-stained traps were put away. Carefully. Certainly don't want nasty old mouse-smelling traps anywhere near any food supplies.

When autumn came again, so did the mice. The traps, stashed with care, could not be found. So more were purchased. And they worked. There were plenty of new fat mice to snap at and, although these traps caught only one mouse at a time, four traps catching four mice per night for seven days equals twenty-eight mice per week. And with four weeks per month . . .

There were special evenings of course. Settled comfortably before the wood stove I'd hear a squeak and a snap before I'd finished chapter one. Remove. Re-set. Chapter two, and another furry creature, having first gobbled up the bait, would perish within the sound of my chair. So, an accurate count isn't possible.

I can't make an accurate count of the number of traps I've purchased either. But somewhere within this rambling farm-house, neatly ensconced in plastic bags, there are eight years of mouse traps. And this week I'll buy some more.

Miss Badger is a super mouser of a dog out of doors. But although she can dig out and dispose of mice with great efficiency in the mulch hay or under the wood pile, she seems to feel that it is unethical to pounce upon a house mouse. We were sitting together on the rug before the stove when we both heard a strange sound. Miss Badger pricked up her ears. (I've never learned that trick.) A rattle? A metallic tapping?

The flange around the pipe bringing water up to the radiator began to vibrate. We watched in silence until a small, bright-eyed mouse face appeared. He (or she?) regarded us, remained motionless with the chrome flange on its back, decided we looked harmless and came forth into the dining room.

"Get him, Badger!"

Miss Badger looked at me as though I'd lost my reason. Attack a house guest?

Now, if you have never chased a small mouse around a large house with a stove poker, you may not exactly understand what went on. But somewhere that small creature is still lurking. She's probably producing yet another generation.

I have this problem? Let's face the issue honestly. I have these problems. Mice do get into old houses. When I put things away, they stay put. This morning there were mouse droppings beside my typewriter. This evening I'll buy more mouse traps. And some day I really will have that second-hand sale.

WE WENT OUT, my dog and I, to walk in the woods again. The hunters have gone. The rains have softened the fallen leaves so the roads and trails are spongy, quiet and elastic underfoot. Miss Badger dashes off in all directions—coming to heel when called—expressing in every bound the pleasure of being down behind the ridge, headed for the swamp.

This woods road is old. An addition to the deed was made in 1861 to give a right of way to a neighbor to haul timber and firewood out from the hill beyond the swamp. Twigs and limbs pruned by the wind litter the woods floor where lichens and green, plush mosses inhabit trees which fell in past years. On every side the natural order of recycling—birth, fruition, death and re-use—continues as it has since the glacier melted from this land. Last month's leaves, wind-drifted against the weathered trunks now sinking into mounds of soft brown dust, give forth an acrid scent of mold and healthy decaying.

The woods are quiet but not silent. Dry seed pods rasp and rattle, scurrying squirrels rustle twigs and leaves, wind in the tree tops moves high limbs to rub against each other. Cheerful chickadees follow down through the woods calling their kind to come and view the visitors. I reward these amiable, energetic birds by knocking bark off a pile of old logs and they swoop in for a feast of ant eggs, larvae and dormant insects.

Beyond the log pile I sit on the stone wall where once a pasture gate swung to let the cows into the south field. Spruce and pine grow there now, their tops high and thick enough to discourage bushes or other undergrowth. From the wall I can see a network of traveled paths under the conifers—just a firmer packing down of the brown needle carpet.

On the north side of the wall abandoned birds' nests are now clearly visible in the hardwoods. Some neat nests are tucked in tidy fashion into the forks of branches. Others, disheveled, sloppy structures with loose leaves flopping like unhinged laundry, hang uneven and ploppy as though declaring that too much effort was deemed unnecessary for just a summer haven. This was good enough for a messy bunch of fledglings.

Below me to the east woodpeckers drum and knock on the trees killed by the backwater of the beaver dam. White stains along the trunk of a tall beech lead me down to look for owl balls, regurgitated bones, fur and tails telling the tales of nocturnal feastings. The owls rest elsewhere on this day, but Miss Badger sniffs and paws, scattering the whitened bones and then bounds off to investigate the smells around a blowdown. I hold my breath, hoping the root hole or browning branches of the fallen tree are not sheltering a family of skunks.

Seven Brook flows through the swamp. Thickets of alders and stunted cedars cluster along both sides. In the past 170 years bridges of varying sorts have been built or tossed up temporarily to span the stream and harvest the timber on the back of Barrett Hill, The run-off from that hill, added to the melting ice and snow in the narrow valley, continues to carry off or splinter every farm-built span. Beaver populations fluctuate, and their flooding changes the growth pattern in the swamp.

Migrating ducks feed in this lowland, and there's a grove of hemlocks with massive roots clutched over a ledge which offers a natural blind for viewing. Badg and I stroll back that way, pushing through the underbrush and the slope thick with slender trees reaching for sunlight. We cross the wood lot road and follow the velvet green path beneath young hemlocks. Water from a hillside spring splashes lightly where it meets the curve of the brook. Sunlight warms the balsams, and the moist air carries the fragrance down to the ledge.

This solitude, these moments of sharp, intense pleasure

in just *being* in the stillness of the woods feed my spirit. Here, with space and time for quiet observing, I'm reminded of the enduring pattern of this earth. The blare of horrors in the TV news, the frustrations of chores not done—these still exist. But walking through the woodlands reminds me that long after I'm gone from this earth, this soil will still host life. The sun will rise and set and the moon will shine upon this land.

There's a wholeness and a holiness of life—a continuity which demands participation. Tranquility and renewed energy surface each time I walk through the quiet woods.

DURING DECEMBER there's a special pleasure in opening my mailbox to find letters from old friends bringing holiday greetings and news of their families and activities. The days of sending out cards with printed signatures seems past. Whether it's the increase in postage or the wisdom which comes with maturity, I don't know, but the messages are personal—letters they cared enough to write and send.

Through the years the news with Christmas greetings has followed a pattern. There were the house hunting stories and then the years of the arrivals of children. All too soon there were the difficulties of college choices and financing and now I'm hearing about grandchildren and plans for retirement.

This year I'm sensing another pattern—a shifting into new careers or changing life styles. Letters with such news are full of vitality and hope. Thirty years ago we were all thinking in terms of working, saving, investing, and then retiring to take it easy—a well-earned rest.

But retiring into puttering has a deadly echo for people who have enjoyed any sense of accomplishment and recognition. One friend writes enthusiastically that he's studying maps of the whole world while planning to devote seven years to service as a medical missionary when he retires as head surgeon at his western hospital. He's busy learning about climates and customs as well as the medical problems of places with strange-sounding names.

Another couple have a small but important tag line on their retirement plans—no more raking leaves. Their plan to build model stage settings doesn't require a specific geographical location so they're vacationing in new areas each year but keeping alert to the deciduous situation. They used to joke about setting up fans in their basement windows to blow the leaves to the next lots. Now they're realistically facing a life style change which includes no drifting of autumn leaves.

Having enough income to retire and begin again is fine but the changes in the economic picture have forced most of my old friends into seeking out new ways to finance the next thirty years. These are the letters I enjoy receiving. When someone who always seemed stodgy and stuck-in-the-mud begins to reach out and find new life in improbable situations, I'm encouraged about the whole human race.

Teaching adults striving for high school credits, driving a bus for senior citizens, pruning shrubs in neighborhood parks, doing surveys in shopping centers—jobs which started as helping out for a few hours have turned into part-time employment. I think I sense a pattern of having to get out and relate to people as one reason my friends have kept going one step further in reaching out beyond their former self-imposed limits.

The threads which have kept me in touch with many of my holiday message senders are woven of some common interest which has not diminished. I look forward to letters with suggestions for books I might like to read or descriptions of visits to cities and islands we once dreamed of seeing. Some letters enclose clippings or cartoons on topics I care about and I have the warm feeling that I am known as a person.

Sometimes it seems as though all the individuals I've met have been winnowed through the sieve of friendship and the ones whose holiday messages come into my mailbox are the prime fruit. Like good fruit, friendships must be nurtured and fed and kept alive with caring. Again—like caring for fruit trees or strawberry plants—each person has limits as to how much can be done richly and well.

There's something about holiday letters which bring out the marshmallow in me. Just looking at the return addresses as I lift them from the mailbox spins me back in time to pleasant hours and, with misty eyes, I stumble over the dog getting into the house to be back in touch.

There's a silly quote someone scrawled in my college yearbook—"People have more fun than anybody!" When the December mail brings letters from across the country and around the world, I know it's true that some people—growing, changing, really alive people—are truly having more fun than anyone.

THIS YEAR perhaps I should hang my head instead of my stocking. Packages of *things* I don't need, however gaily they are wrapped in holiday papers. But *ideas* I could use. Ideas and facts and lots of intangible virtues.

Years ago an English teacher explained that intangibles were those things you couldn't chase down the street, capture, and put into a box. So they're not found on Christmas lists nor in holiday catalogs.

But I'm feeling that these intangibles are what I'm wanting and needing. I'm even believing that they're what the whole celebration is about.

Faith and trust in my fellow human beings. I could use a fresh measure of that or a toning up of what I've been using. When I sit back and think about the people I know, I'm convinced that those who live with faith in their fellow men are the successful ones. I don't mean financial wealth. I mean living with a sense of joy, being able to duck through the waves of adversity and come up swimming strongly forward.

Patience. That would be a welcome gift especially if it came festooned with bits of humor. I feel a definite lowering in my capacity for viewing the world with a healthy sense of humor when the temperature dips. Getting about takes longer on icy roads. Waiting seems doubly irritating and wasteful with cold toes.

Fortitude and endurance would be helpful also if this is going to be a winter of climatic severity. Thermal underwear I have. What I'm wishing for is a better attitude toward life while I'm padded out in layers of winter clothing.

I'd like to find plentiful portions of kindness and consideration tucked inside myself so that they would rub off on others as baby blanket lint rubs off on dark sweaters. Instead of awakening on Christmas morning to a stocking stuffed and bulging, I'd like to find within me some gifts of awareness. An increased ability to hear what others are saying—not just by their words but with their tone, and posture, and gestures.

You can't walk into a super market and say "Empathy—the large size please." Someone would call the manager. Yet each year the Christmas message repeats man's need for the empathic heart.

Lighted Christmas trees are special. The color, the brightness, the glow, bring back belief in the magic of this holiday. All wishes might come true.

Could I wish for some instant insight and enlightenment about taxes? The Internal Revenue Service got their mailings out this year before the first Christmas card senders. It will take a bit of magic plus a gift of mathematical expertise to figure out what to pay or not pay in the next two weeks to make the April-due payments less.

Certainly I can wish for an active supply of winter birds. Already they're chirping about my neighbor's feeders while ignoring my sunflower seeds. I have no lurking cats, and according to the books, pine groves are the kind of shelter such birds seek.

If I'm going to ask for ideas this Christmas—fresh, stimulating ideas—I'd better add an extra request for the courage to accept and use them. Each time I'm offered a new challenge professionally I find myself backing off with doubts of my ability to accept and accomplish.

The feeling of Christmas is in the mind and in the heart but the visible symbols—the lighted trees, the carols, the gifts and cards—are reminders of the promise of this birthday. Woven into the traditions of our Christmas celebrations is a new lift to our lives, renewed hope for good will.

Perhaps it's because this celebration comes when the nights are longest and the daylight hours shortened, when the gray cold has settled in, that it becomes a time of rediscovery.

While this planet begins to turn toward longer days and springtime, we gather together. The bright lights and music push back the darkness and the spirit of Christmas moves in.

OLD SCROOGE had his ghosts of past Christmases to shake him up and help him see how to appreciate the present. My books of Christmases past accomplish somewhat the same function but they stay around, accumulating and rubbing covers with each other.

Kate Douglas Wiggin's sentimental tale of the delicate, golden-haired Christmas child celebrating Christ's birthday was first published in 1896. There are some old-fashioned asides to "dear reader" but these do not obscure the verbal pictures of Mrs. Ruggles's valiant attempts to get her nine noisy children cleaned up and outfitted to dine with the wealthy Bird family. My copy of The Birds' Christmas Carol is worn and tattered but each year my sympathy goes out to poor Sarah Maud who has the responsibility for monitoring the social graces of the Ruggles brood.

There is a rule of thumb: "If you haven't opened the book in three years, you can get along without it." Rational perhaps, but ignoring nostalgia. James Stephens' Crock of Gold probably hasn't been opened in six years, yet each time I dust I run my finger along its spine and remember the Christmas we quoted the Philosophers who were able to hear each other thinking all day long. Yes, and I still feel like calling some people "lob-eared, crock-kneed fat-eyes."

The Christmas books tell more stories than can be found between their covers. In just holding them some of the pleasure comes bubbling back and in rereading I can capture some of the feelings of the particular holiday that gift became mine.

Probably I was eleven when L. M. Montgomery's The Blue Castle appeared under my Christmas tree. The heroine, utterly dominated by a clan of stuffy relatives, secretly consults a doctor. Before he can give her his diagnosis, he is called away.

When a letter from the doctor informs her that she has only one year to live, our heroine decides that for that year she will do only what seems right to her. She will stop pretending, stop trying to please others, and always tell the truth. This she proceeds to do, even asking a mysterious stranger to marry her and going off to live in his island cabin.

Pretty heady stuff for an eleven-year-old (in those days), romantic and full of leads for personal daydreams. I can now reread this novel in about two hours, gathering in some of the delight I first felt as the twenty-nine-year-old heroine began to tell the truth to her domineering relatives. And woven into the romantic tale are some basic messages. People-pleasing is corrosive. Learning to be honest makes it possible to grow as a human being. Loving someone encompasses trust and acceptance. Life without laughter is mere existence. Those are good gifts for any age.

Mary Ellen Chase's *The Bible and the Common Reader* was a gift the year I agreed to teach a course vaguely termed "An Overall View of the Bible." I kept about two weeks ahead of my classes, reading avidly. Chase's book, which grew out of her experiences in teaching the Bible at Smith College, taught me to slow down, to ponder, and to focus on my students' questions. When I think of the 300 years of writing and rewriting before the New Testament was finalized and put into circulation, I ponder about the editing and the manuscripts which were rejected. For, as anyone dealing with words knows, editors—however dedicated and inspired— are human.

Reuel Robinson's *History of Camden and Rockport* started my collection of local history references. Not new, a treasured family copy, this gift came complete with penciled notes and yellowed clippings tucked in as bookmarks. Almost every holiday since then has added another book on Maine history.

Stuart Little dates back to the lab Christmas tree during medical research years. Eight thoughtful people gave the gift they'd like to receive—and we all ended up with Stuart! I don't know E. B. White's intent when he wrote this fantasy of the second son who looked very much like a mouse, but for us—the young men and women from five different states—the acceptance of Stuart's differences was something with which we could identify. Involved in figuring out what we wanted to do with our lives, trying to understand the ways our ethnic backgrounds and home locales influenced our values, we found E. B. White's philosophical character ready to help us begin to really talk.

Ogden Nash doesn't mention Christmas in his poem about Belinda and her realio, trulio, little pet dragon but because we always read that along with Jabez Dawes and his denunciations of Santa Claus, I think of Belinda at Christmas time. New Nash books were always welcome under the tree to add to the repertoire of verses about the aberrations and anomalies of being human.

No Christmas is complete without books and unhassled time to delve into them. Libraries can supply the "read it once" kind of books but Christmas volumes should be transports to other worlds—magic carpets of fast flowing words to carry one away again and again.

Like well chosen friends, books add to my living.

JANUARY

J A N U A R Y is named for the Roman God, Janus, the one with two faces. Because he could look two ways at once, he represented wisdom. Being able to view the past while facing the future or looking inward while contemplating the outer world, old Janus probably started the idea of New Year's resolutions.

I've given up this end of the year practice. There's something so stiltingly noble and unrealistic about most lists of resolutions that the only human response is "Whom are you kidding?" Besides, making such detailed plans to be a better person suggests that one has been operating as a general nerd for the past twelve months. Why would anyone want to end the year with such a negative kind of thinking?

Trying to remember to write the correct date on my checks and to shift taxable records into a new file folder reminds me that a new year is starting. But I don't really feel a newness or a sense of beginning again until the frost comes out of the ground and the earth comes back to growing life. The new year should start with March—not more cold days and nights.

Instead of resolutions, I prefer to think in terms of new ventures possible in the next 365 days. What do I want to learn? What places do I want to visit? What new experiences do I want to get involved in? Here Janus's two faces present a good image. What did I accomplish in the past year which will influence my plans for next year?

Friends, good friends, began to remind me that my conversation was frequently peppered with the phrase, "Someday I'm going to . . ." and to ask when I thought someday would arrive. With the removal of each calendar page during this year, I became more aware of how many people of my acquaintance could no longer plan for active adventures in the future. I experimented with a new phrase, "Why not now?"

Flying out to Matinicus shifted from a someday dream to

a July reality. It's one thing to look at a map of the coast of Maine and see the dots of islands. It's quite another to fly over them. Looking down from the mail plane their green and rocky abundance seems incredible. The rocks and ridges visible under the water gave me a new respect for the skill and seamanship of summer sailors and coastal fishermen.

Matinicus does not cater to tourists. I stayed with my friend, Gladys Mitchell, who was not only born on the island but is a direct descendant of the first settler, Ebenezer Hall, killed by Indians in 1757. These Indians objected to Hall's planting two of their tribe in his garden.

Exploring Matinicus by walking the roads and beaches was doubly pleasurable because Mrs. Mitchell's stories gave me the history as well as the current problems and issues of island living. Years ago I had quoted Milton Carleton in an article on rhubarb as an invulnerable root carried into new frontiers. On the island I had the opportunity to talk with him and to comment on his common sense writings about home gardening.

During the summer and fall I parked my hoe, covered my typewriter and took off to visit other islands. Boat trips to Monhegan and Islesboro gave me a chance to see a good part of the local coast and the islands from a new perspective. Boarding at Tenant's Harbor and consulting the maps as we progressed, I found I was mentally checking off a whole list of "Someday I'm going to . . ." items.

Rock-picking while waiting for the clams to steam re-minded me of the power of the glaciers which tumbled so many different parts of the earth's surface together. The tides of thousands of years have continued this tossing and tum-bling so that each handful of stones upon the beach presents variety unlimited. Finding stress lines or cracks in these samples and—with larger rocks—cracking them was a min-iature demonstration of how the sands and soils were formed.

On Monhegan the deer showed no fear as they nibbled

flower borders along the road to the wharf or tried to circumvent fences around lettuce patches with an audience of dozens. Matinicus is without deer, foxes, coons, and such wildlife. But I was glad to hear that some years ago frogs had been imported so the islanders could enjoy that welcome sound of spring.

Like Janus I can look back on pleasant excursions and think ahead to more islands to visit. Editors have been receptive during the year so I can keep working on the kinds of writing I enjoy. Having all the children and grandchildren on the farm for Christmas was delightful and the promise of a new grandson next May was a special gift for the coming year.

Perhaps this two-faced god represents wisdom because his looking inward and outward suggests pausing often to be more aware of the *now*. A year is a segment on a spiral, repeated but never identical. So is each day. And each hour. I hope I can keep remembering this.

W HEN I FOUND myself tabulating the number of days until the spring equinox, it was time to do something. Wishing winter away is wasteful, downright sinful, like sitting in a closet hoping life will get more exciting.

Slipping into boots and jacket I went forth into the January sunshine. After the bone chilling cold of last week it was a pleasure to be outside shoveling the mailbox clear again. No icy winds. No drifting snow. The white cover across the lawn and gardens cushioned the farm in silence.

Silence? From across the pond the rumble of a heavy truck faded away; the chickadees in the hemlock windbreak chirped cheerfully; Miss Badger with doggish abandon chased herself in circles beyond the rhubarb patch. My hilltop had a comfortable stillness—an absence of noises.

Until my ailing knee is repaired I have to forego snow-shoeing so I just strolled along the road looking at my snow-covered acres. The apple and pear trees need pruning. Outlined against the white field they have a raggle-taggle neglected appearance. The winds during the last snowfall passed around these trees to form uneven drifts. Even the weed stalks along the fence row had diverted that wind so that miniature drifts built up beyond them.

Learning to identify trees by their leafless outlines is on my winter list. Because I'm already familiar with many trees on my acres, this learning sounded simple. The branches of maple trees grow upward, oak limbs grow outward, and those of the ash are opposite each other.

But strolling down the road under trees I know are maples, I find variations, non-conformists, even among those planted along the south field. Some folks claim that the run-off of road salt during the last twenty years has warped the growth patterns of roadside trees but these maples look as though they had rebelled against symmetrical growth long before any salt was used on this road.

The reference books I've been reading are helpful, but

confusing. About the time I think I should be able to recognize a tree by its winter silhouette, stark and bare against the sky, I find the small print:

"The shape of this tree will vary if grown in the open and it may be ten feet taller under favorable conditions."

My sole surviving, still healthy elm fits the book classification of umbrella top. The magnificent vase-shaped elms are gone. The trunk of the largest elm, now prone like a fallen giant, needs to be sawed up and hauled off so that field can be reseeded. This stump measures nineteen feet around. Various people have sawed and hacked at it when in need of firewood but such a monster is not easy to work up.

That elm had a different shape with great branches growing out instead of skyward as the vase elms did. Some illustrations of the English elm picture such a silhouette. But how would one English elm get rooted before a barn on this road? I wonder where the orioles which nested there each year have found another haven.

Looking at the patterns of trees along my land, I realize I have never seen a *grove* of elm trees. There were a dozen along the base of the pine ridge and a clump of four down by the muskrat meadow—but no acre of elms. Although I've heard and read about a tradition of planting two elms—a male tree and a female tree—in front of new homes as gifts for the bride and groom, not one of my reference books even hints at the sex of the elms.

Pines are thick over many acres. Hemlocks and spruce cover large areas and the great oaks border the pond. Other trees—beech, birch, ash and poplar—seem more gregarious and scatter themselves in mixed growth.

The squat oak, which has for years reached its chunky branches out to scratch all passing trucks, has succumbed to parasites and is being cut for firewood. This tree grew out like a heavy armed octopus and provided splendid branches for climbing except for the danger of falling onto a passing car. But it just didn't grow up. It huddled beside the road.

Trees have personalities. I find I'm accustomed to enjoying their sight and shape and responses to hilltop winds. When they're gone, it's like adapting to a lost tooth.

I need more knowledge about the color, texture, and patterns of bark. More effort in sketching will help. I don't expect to become an expert but practicing winter tree identification while strolling in the fresh air is far more positive than wishing the winter away.

THE HEMLOCK windbreak is decorated with blue jays. Their feathers fluffed for extra insulation, a dozen or so birds look like blue and white snowballs caught among the green boughs. While an icy wind gusts down through the valley, the ruffled jays perch in the hemlocks facing the morning sun.

A movement on the back steps catches my eye. Small Red, paws folded close to his chest, is warily watching the dog. The wind spreads the hairs in the small squirrel's tail but he moves only his head as those white-rimmed eyes watch Miss Badger's sniffing check of the compost pile. This may or may not be the same red squirrel I watched last winter but he has taken up the same residence in my garage wood-pile, demonstrated the same ability to scamper up the clapboards to the birdfeeder, and appears upon the living room window sill to take his turn at watching me.

Last year many people warned me about red squirrels. Yes, they're cute to watch—cheerful, chattering, curious little auburn-furred creatures. But they carry rabies. If they get into your attic, you'll never get rid of them. Red squirrels are worse than bats. They chew up everything and raise more little rodents to roam through the rafters. Every old husband tale ever repeated in this valley was dredged up to discourage my pleasure in just observing Small Red.

Come spring he disappeared. I found no evidence of gnawing vandalism in the workshop over the garage nor in the shed behind it so, with his return this month, I'm enjoying his feeding forages. Miss Badger ignores him. Perhaps she bumped her nose too often trying to pursue him under the car or into the stacked firewood. Badg growls if Small Red attempts to approach the bird feeder while the dog is sunning herself on the lawn and the squirrel takes a cautious look around before leaving the safety of the garage.

Rabbits in their thick, white, winter fur can be seen along the edges of these acres but they stay away from the area which Miss Badger patrols in her daily farm wanderings. One fox has been sighted trotting purposefully down along the south field headed for the marsh below Katy Cove. How much careful scrutiny this red-coated animal made before crossing the road, I don't know, but observed through the field glasses the fox appeared relaxed and unconcerned.

From the farmhouse windows I can look in all directions and view the dormant acres, the contours smoothed and free of disguising vegetation. Movements of birds or small animals are easier to spot while the frost holds the earth rigid. While the land rests and some wild creatures hibernate, others are engaged in a continual seeking for food and this is a time for watching.

When the land is covered with snow—even a light dusting of white flakes—the autographs of small creatures can be read. Using a pancake turner it's possible to collect a few sets of tracks and keep them in the freezer to show the grandchildren or to find confirmation of identification.

Where were the voles before my late December banking of the house? Immediately they appear and settle in to dry, cozy nests. Where the chickadees scatter seeds, the voles burrow out through snow tunnels to feed. With a sudden thaw their network of traffic lanes shows up. Just as human steps and dog tracks across a snowy lawn will pack a trail of ice, the travels of these feather-weight creatures—and perhaps the warmth of their fur-covered bellies sliding along the earth—form miniature communication lanes out from the hay bales.

The midday sun—even in January—melts and distorts tracks in the snow. One year I sighted a large bobcat crossing the east field but didn't go out until the next day to observe and measure the tracks. Being, at that time, unaware of the size changes caused by the sun, I was sure a full-sized panther had moved into my woods.

The January landscape may appear bleak and barren but

a slow stroll across the fields and down into the woods provides evidence of the winter habits of many tenants upon my acres. Like the jays which fluff themselves into round balls of blue and white, survival patterns are there to be read. Track reading as well as field glass watching are wintertime projects which increase my understanding of my country environment. And add to marveling anew at the awesome aspects of the intertwining lives within sight of my own home windows.

LAST WEEK I planted five telephone directories in the rhubarb bed. For twenty-five years I've been disposing of catalogs, junk mail, and magazines in this garden, covering them with hay and manure and letting the earthworms return them to the soil.

This isn't usually a January task. However when I had trouble closing the drawer where the phone book is kept, I did some early housecleaning. Each spring when the new directory arrives I intend to promptly copy out those write-in numbers and notes, but procrastination prevails.

When someone moves or gets a different number, I ink in their name and number at the top of the correct alphabetical page. That's efficient. But in those '77 to '81 books there are names of people I don't recall knowing. And some telephone numbers without names. I almost gave in to an impulse to dial a few of those. Just say "This Arley Clark. Who are you?"

In skimming before pitching I did find the directions for calling someone on my own party line. This is good. The last time a neighbor's dog got loose and came to visit, I had to phone someone in the village to call my neighbor because the on-line system of your digit plus my digit plus some neutral number and hang up fast directions weren't in my memory nor in the '82 directory. Now if I will just take time to write the phone company to find out who is currently on my party line in case I should want to call them . . .

I think there are four parties on my line now. When we moved here there were twenty-two. In an emergency you just politely asked for the line. Listening-in was accepted practice and only caused problems when six or seven people did it at the same time. This somehow lowered the tone volume. It also made long distance calls difficult, longer and more expensive because everything had to be shouted over and over.

This aspect of rural telephoning we learned when—ten

days after moving into the farmhouse—I went off to the hospital to have a premature baby and my husband called his mother to tell her the news. The more he shouted the glad tidings, the lower the volume became until it was necessary to have the operator relay the message. Four days later, by U.S. mail, we learned that grandma had never received the call. Some unknown woman somewhere in Maine heard via the operator that she had a lovely new granddaughter named Kate.

Looking back I think I can understand some of the curiosity of the party line folks at that time. Most of them had heard about new people "from away" moving in and had been watching the farmhouse as they drove slowly past. The woman from up-country who was helping me unpack was rather round—especially in the middle. Temperatures were in the 90s. Finally she declared that she was going to remove her corsets and added, "I just don't care how I look in this heat. Let the neighbors think that man from New Jersey has two wives and they're both pregnant."

In those days the telephone was a big crank job hung on the wall and the local operators gave more than directory assistance. They gave directions to the town dump and to the first selectman's house. They not only offered suggestions on who could fix things but knew whose farm they were working on that day. When we had a boy from the Bronx staying here under the *Herald Tribune* Fresh Air Fund, I rang the operator to find someone going from this village to the Catholic church. That time there was a thoughtful pause and then the information that there was only one Catholic in town and she didn't go to church. I was also informed that only one Democrat lived in town.

The old phone was a lightning attractor. The blue arcs around the wallbox and across the kitchen were spectacular. No telephone since has performed as brilliantly, although each improved model has carried on the tradition of going dead in the midst of storms. This isn't a problem unless you *know* it's out of order. It's quite possible to sit out blizzards and hurricanes, just looking at the phone and feeling secure. No trees have crashed through the roof in the past 170 years.

I like the tidy feeling of having an organized phone directory and space in that kitchen drawer. Now if I could just overcome my extreme reluctance (phobia?) about using the phone and figure out why inserting my key in the front door sets this instrument ringing . . . With eighty pounds of dog prancing in welcome, my hands full of mail, and my arms full of stuff, I never manage a "Hello" before there's a click.

But didn't I read about innovative technology for home phones? A cordless phone beside the welcome mat? Cartridges with memory banks of frequently used numbers? It's possible that Ma Bell or one of her spin-offs may someday give us something to equal those human operators who could locate a plumber, a Baptist or a Democrat.

W H E N I F I R S T set foot in the Pine Tree State in 1943, after an overnight journey on the State of Maine Express, I had no idea that some of my ancestors had been eating lobster here before 1650.

Delving into family history started some fifteen years later when my son, John Rogers Clark IV, came home with a fifth-grade assignment to find information about an ancestor. Several of his classmates had already declared that they had famous war heroes among their great-grandfathers and John wanted someone equally notable.

Very simple. Nothing to it. I told him that on his father's side he was a direct descendant of John Churchill, the first Duke of Marlborough. Remember all those Churchill graves in that cemetery where grandpa is buried? And your mother is a descendant of John Paul Jones, one of America's great naval heroes.

Although my son was born in New Jersey, the Maine air brought forth a Yankee core of shrewdness. His immediate reply was, "Prove it."

I dug out some family records inherited from an aunt who had died at age eighty-seven and found the newspaper clippings of great grandma's death with bold headlines proclaiming her a direct descendant of that first duke. If it's in the paper, it must be so. But let's look a little further.

The encyclopedia informed us that one John Churchill had in 1702 been given that title for his meritorius service at the Battle of Blenheim. Alas. Our ancestor, John Churchill, had been living in Plymouth, Mass. before his marriage in 1644. For more than one hundred years family members had been passing along a story which had no basis in fact.

What about John Paul Jones? We started with the encyclopedia instead of great-grandmother's familiar admonition, "Don't do anything to disgrace the family. Remember you are a descendant of a great American."

John Paul Jones never married. Many excellent historians

have documented his adult life but despite his reputation as a charming ladies' man in France, England, and in his own country, there's not even a hint of any offspring. So much for family tales.

My son went back to school with notes on one Revolutionary ancestor who had three wives and seventeen children including quadruplets Washington, Warren, Madison and Ruth. I went back to studying those old records.

Figuring a generation as twenty-five years and taking the Mayflower arrival as an arbitrary date, I estimated that in that period of time my kids had 16,384 ancestors. Two parents, four grandparents, eight great-grandparents, etc. for fourteen generations. Surely out of such abundance I could discover a few ancestors of note.

This became an engrossing hobby. However, the serendipity of sire searching proved more intriguing than finding claims to illustrious men of history. Tracking down ancestors involved learning about economic changes, religious movements, and immigration patterns.

Money, seeking ways to earn a better living, and need for more land set families to move on. When there were more than a dozen children, the homestead couldn't support the next generation. When the Huguenots fled persecution in France they found brides in the Hudson River settlements and hustled them off to new lands along the Delaware River.

Much has been written about Sir William Phips, the first native-born Colonial Governor of New England, but little is on record about his stepfather. Shortly after little William was born about 1651 his father died. Since this lad was her twenty-first child, most folks would agree that widow Mary Phips did need another husband to provide for her and hers in the Maine wilderness. My ancestor, John White, having lost his wife, upped and married the widow. She was so grateful for his masculine support that she proceeded to present him with five children.

Try to visualize the life of this family in those days. In the 1650s what would one use for diapers? For footwear for all those children? And when the tiny cabin became too noisy and crowded and one wanted to send them out for a bit of fresh air, what would twenty-six youngsters wear for jackets? What kind of kettles were used by the open hearth to cook for such a brood?

John White rowed across Merrymeeting Bay on May 23, 1654 to join the heads of the other fifteen families within the Kennebec Grant, to pledge allegiance to the Plymouth Colony, and to organize a local civil government for mutual protection. The Indians ignored this pact when they burned the homes in 1676. John and Mary sailed off to Boston and safety but as soon as things calmed down, John White returned. Indians or not—Maine was home.

I've heard remarks about those "from away" for more than three decades. John White probably didn't have to deal with this when he sailed in from Bristol, England, but the natives communicated that idea when they burned his Jeremesquam home. Three hundred years later I understand his return. Maine is home.

THE OLD-TIMERS brought forth their stories about blizzards in this valley each time anyone "from away" complained about the winter storms. They told about tunneling through drifts to get to the barn and how in years past piles of snow were still snug against the north sides of buildings on May Day.

One year, I was told, the drifts in front of my farmhouse were so high that the men plowed out (or was it rolled down?) a detour around behind the barn and up through the blueberry field. They didn't find East Sennebec Road again until April.

These tales of rugged blizzards usually included the story of the woman who lived alone on Clarry Hill with dozens of cats. After one long-lasting storm with drifts which blocked all doorways, someone snowshoed up to her place. Poor Sadie had perished. Her starving pets had put survival before loyalty.

Driving through snow storms leaves me feeling as though I'd just given three blood transfusions. No matter which route I take, I can't get out of town and back home without facing at least one big hill. If there's a storm, there are cars slithered crosswise halfway up or down those hills. I find myself talking to my car the way my grandmother used to talk to her horse, coaxing her on, praising her steadiness, and shouting encouragement as we gently skirt the stalled vehicles and climb on up the hill.

The first—and the best—advice given to me about winter driving was offered by an old-timer who rescued me about a month after I got my first driver's license. My multiple attempts to get up over the Town House Hill (the only direct way out of the village in those days) were observed with interest by the men socializing in the local garage.

Finally I went into the garage to ask when the sanding truck might be along. No one knew but they did express the opinion that with *good* driving that hill was not a hazard. I wasn't about to put on another backsliding exhibition. I stood quietly thinking very evil thoughts until at last one of the old-timers allowed as how it would be neighborly if he got my car up the hill for me.

After he had backed down four times (aware of the audience) he volunteered to drive me home in his car by the alternate route up the other side of the river. Enroute he gave me advice on driving in Maine winters.

"Now, comes weather like this you just make believe you got a dozen eggs right there on the seat beside you and you drive so they don't fall off."

"I wasn't driving carelessly," I protested, "and a box of eggs . . ."

"Lady," my instructor said gently, "them eggs ain't in no box."

Many dozens of imaginary eggs have ridden beside me through stormy winters. Advice worth remembering.

But if I don't have to venture forth, I like blizzards. I think of them as a warp in time—a period of unallotted hours. Freedom from musts and shoulds and any kinds of chores. Usually I mix some bread dough because I enjoy the kneading and the aroma of the baking loaves. I read, take naps, dig out some old 78 records, thaw some strawberries and asparagus—just let go and enjoy my own company.

Blizzard days were a pleasure when the children were in school because we all took a bit of that "this day is a gift" attitude. From the upstairs bedroom we would drag down the Blizzard Box which contains years of clipping of recipes from newspapers and magazines.

First we'd just rummage through talking and thinking about something different to eat. Then we'd start setting a few aside to try someday. Eventually we'd find a few too good to miss and start cooking. Many of our family favorites (preserved in the Good Book of Tested Recipes) were discovered and tried out during raging northeast storms. The box went back looking as full as ever but it was a delightful way to share a few housebound hours.

Most of the old-timers who told of blizzards past are no longer around—but their tales remain part of the legends of this valley. Perhaps their storms really were worse or longer. Or it may be that they settled in and enjoyed them and wove yarns to pass along to newcomers to Georges Valley.

When a blizzard can be—like a vacation—a suspension of regular activities in order to rest and refresh one's mind and body, it adds a lift to the weeks of winter.

FEBRUARY

W I T H O U T a protective covering of snow, my kitchen garden lies exposed, and puddles of water show me where more compost and old manure should be added. But by comparing this February's resting soil with photos of the same garden ten years ago, I can realize how much I've learned about soil and slopes and spacing.

This comparison and observation of the vegetable garden has been part of trying to answer a letter from a friend who is moving to a small town and wants to know how to begin gardening. What simple practical suggestions should I offer? Every bookstore has rows of gardening books, most of them illustrated with bright photos of carefully cultivated, productive plots and charts of what to plant where. The trouble for many beginners is that each book seems to recommend something different, and many are so full of how-to-do-it paragraphs that they make raising carrots seem to be as complicated as learning to fly a 747.

Therefore I want my suggestions to be brief—only a few, and those simple and encouraging. Most knowledge of growing vegetables or flowers is acquired by trial and effort, and if the beginnings are small there's more opportunity to enjoy the learning.

A vegetable garden needs sun for at least six hours each day, so where to begin involves openness and a thought to how any buildings will throw shadows during the summer months. It's difficult to remember how trees—bare and slender in February—will look when once again they are in full leaf, shading large areas.

Having the ground plowed and tilled—no matter how small the planned plot—is almost always money well invested. Blisters and backaches resulting from turning sod can discourage gardeners, and the new garden tillers do a great job of pulverizing the big roots. Good tilling in the beginning means easier regular care. After a few years of cultivation, no mechanical tilling may be needed, but for beginning it's a prudent plan to use machines instead of muscles.

Less path, more plants might be another suggestion. Single, skinny rows require much more hoeing and all the ground which gets walked upon gets compacted. The earthworms which keep the soil full of air vents and which ingest organic matter and pass out nutrient rich particles can't operate well in packed down earth. Wide rows—a yard stick is a good measure—mean more plants and less weeding because the scatter planted vegetables grow to shade each other's roots.

What to plant? Perhaps to encourage the beginning gardener each choice should be vegetables which cannot be purchased in a supermarket or which, in a market, cannot have the texture and flavor found in freshly-picked vegetables. Cucumbers, green beans, peas, chard, leeks, carrots and leaf lettuce are in this grouping. Don't give space in a small garden to potatoes, onions or winter squash which do not depend upon absolute freshness for quality and flavor. But peas picked thirty minutes before dinner *are* different.

Plants which produce over a long period should encourage a beginning gardener—maximum production for the time, effort and space. Leaf lettuce instead of head lettuce. New Zealand spinach, which provides greens until frost, instead of garden spinach which seldom provides enough for more than two meals and then bolts. Planning for a continuous harvesting makes gardening more worthwhile.

Small doesn't mean limited. A few parsley plants, several green basils and a bit of dill along the edge provide taste treats all season long. Replanting after harvesting means more production within a small plot. Pole beans and poles for cucumbers mean more produce in a limited soil area.

My gardening philosophy—it's better to plant just one cauliflower than never to have planted at all—has led me to encouraging people to plant just one tub or one square yard to watch the growth. Enjoying the variety and crispness of garden vegetables has led me to experimenting and thus learning about new foods as well as knowledge about gardening.

So my suggestions to a beginning gardener will be limited. I want to encourage but not confuse, make it seem a pleasure and not another work project. Begin small but begin. Keep a garden small enough to enjoy but get maximum production through choice of seeds and wide row planting. Take advantage of labor-saving machines but be there with a weeder and a hoe to participate in the growing season. Plan for pleasure—the best harvest from any garden.

FEBRUARY'S SUN is brighter, stronger. Each weed stem has absorbed enough heat to melt a hole around it, giving the field an embroidered pattern. Along the pine ridge each tree stands in its own dark pocket while in the back yard the melt holes around the post legs of the soil-sifter suggest that the clumsy thing just jumped down into the snow wearing size thirteen galoshes.

The jeering of the blue jays has a less raucous tone as they welcome more of their relatives back to the shelter of the hemlocks. The gray squirrels, continuing their mating chases, seem to fly off snowbanks heeding neither cars, dogs nor strolling humans. There's a fresh scent of skunk in the garage, voles are feeding on bird seed by the dining room window, and a rat ran across the front steps in midafternoon. Not all signs of spring are joyful.

When I look down across the kitchen garden space, I find I'm seeing it in squares. A kind of mental grid imposes itself, dividing the area. This year's planning and planting must be different because I've had to re-order my personal priorities for summer use of time and energy. But—in spite of facing those facts—I keep regarding that 1,600 square feet of space knowing that if I do not plant this, something will grow there. And it probably will not be what I want to see or mow or have next to my vegetables. Nature will not let this soil remain fallow.

My attitude toward this small bit of earth is not always rational or logical. At times I have reacted like a kid with her first tricycle—"Don't touch it. It's mine, mine, *mine!*" In this soil I did my first planting, made my first mistakes and learned. My garden diary for those first years sometimes reads like a green comedy of horticultural idiocy. Elemental errors like neglecting to mark or label where or what I had planted and—one weekend later—tenderly sowing carrots in the row where I had already planted leeks.

I made a joke of that. Insisted I had planted a "soup row."

But as I knelt in the garden with a book picturing seedlings in one hand and a magnifying glass in the other, the tiny spears breaking evenly through the ground pointed up how much I had to learn.

In recent years I've felt a warm pride in the production from this garden. Smug and humble at the same time—if such feelings can co-exist. Perhaps it's a bit like Spencer Tracy in "Boy's Town": taking on a lot of problems, hearing that it can't be done, knowing you didn't do it without some heavenly help, but giving in to the right to feel pride in achieving. While I have enjoyed the lush growth of more recent summers, I have not forgotten the rubbish and weed-choked site it used to be.

During an interview recently I was asked to give two important bits of advice for new home gardeners. This required an immediate response but, after considering what I answered, I believe that if I'd had thirty-six hours to ponder, my reply would not have been much different.

First, gardeners must start with the soil which is there. I cringe whenever I read articles (yes, articles edited, published and paid for) which suggest that if one buys the right seed, plants it just so deep and waters well, all will be perfect. Too many new home gardeners start out with thin top soil some contractor has spread over gravel, trash or ledge. Or they begin on bits of land which have been misused or overplanted for decades.

Second, every gardener needs to be reminded and reminded that soil needs to be nourished, safe-guarded, cared for. This thin layer of earth supports life—it's vital to the survival of practically every living creature and plant. Whether it's in a backyard garden in Maine or a 1,000-acre corn field in Iowa, the stewardship of the land is important. Human beings continue to reproduce themselves beyond what this planet can sustain and to cover crop lands with housing developments. When I look at aerial views of suburbs spread across former farmland, I wonder what happened to the soil removed from those thousands of cellar holes.

My students laughed at me for years because I rolled up my banana peels and replaced them in my lunch bag to carry home to my garden. Some have even gone around the cafeteria collecting banana peels to see my reaction. In seventeen years I've added many peels and other organic materials which will break down into compost. I believe it is this regular, continued adding which makes the earthworms and microorganisms here on Sennebec Hill so willing to help my gardens grow.

If I've learned nothing else from my gardening on these acres, I now care about and for the land. And the more I learn about my own soil and crop yields, the more I believe that preserving prime farmland should be our top priority in national security. Meanwhile, I'll continue to feed the microorganisms right in my own backyard and to encourage others to do the same.

M I D W I N T E R   F U N K begins at 3 p.m. on Sunday. Some doctors, social workers and psychologists have already taken trips south to soak up sunshine and fresh fruit supplements so they'll have the energy to cope with the anxiety attacks this season brings to their offices.

Cabin fever, which often begins as early as Jan. 10, is usually treated with the advice to either get out of the cabin or invite some fellow human beings in.

But with the advent of the midwinter funk period, many northern residents have reached the point of snarling at their most congenial friends and mewling about fears of running out of wood, money and enough energy to get out of bed in the morning. Although medical textbooks neither list this seasonal malady nor suggest specific treatments, most people who have spent more than two winters north of latitude 42 begin to avoid slack-jawed, bent-shouldered neighbors who only want to moan about the misery of winter.

During these weeks when—as the old almanacs stated— "Days lengthen; cold strengthens," other citizens dash forth to scale ice-covered cliffs, race snowmobiles across frozen ponds or just waddle about layered in down-filled garments exclaiming, "Isn't this invigorating?"

Between the anxious and the active are the "snugged-in" types—those who have been anticipating these winter weeks. They don't enjoy driving on icy roads but accept such inconveniences as a natural part of winter. And in accepting the fact that winter *does* exist and the weather sometimes *is* nasty, these folks settle down to celebrate the season.

Looking forward to winter weeks seems to start with an attitude toward the whole cycle of seasons. Spring planting and summer harvesting provide foods for February meals. The messy peeling and cleaning was done before the freezing and canning. If, during those preparatory activities, pleasant thoughts of being snugged-in with plenty to eat were allowed to expand and grow, the confinement by weather can be a welcome reward—planned leisure with time to relax and think.

There's an up-country story about a friendly couple who moved up from the city and after a winter storm decided to call on a neighbor whom they heard lived alone. The neighbor was not grateful. No, he didn't need anything. And he did not care to be interrupted. "I been just waiting for a slow-down storm so's I could get acquainted with myself again. February's my reckoning time."

Could it be that some of the discontent and unrest associated with midwinter funk periods comes from avoiding a time of reckoning and getting acquainted with one's self?

Celebrating winter as a time to settle in and relax, a time to indulge in some of the "someday I'm going to . . ." activities, tends to make the weeks fly by. A special pile of books reserved to dip into, another good try at sketching the starkness of white birches against a clump of pines, updating family albums and genealogical records or learning to play a recorder can be personal rewards.

Midwinter is a time for cooking sprees—for trying something new. With the stoves pouring out heat, the sourdough starter can be reactivated while reading tales of the Old West and the Yukon gold rush when the prospectors were called "sourdoughs" because they carried their wild yeast cultures inside their shirts to keep it bubbling. Kneading a batch of sourdough pumpernickel dark with a bit of bitter chocolate and rye and whole wheat flours can bring back memories of other breads tasted in far away places.

Peppercorns—once so highly prized they changed the course of history—are reputed to aid digestion and dispositions. Yeast bread with onions and a full teaspoon of freshly ground black pepper will fill a winter house with aromas. Peppercorns crushed roughly (hammer whacked within a plastic bag) and patted into steak for a lively steak au poivre deserves a place with February taste treats.

Individual reactions to cold and to confinement when weather discourages driving can be irritability, unrest or pleasure and probably the mind-set was programmed while fitting in the storm windows last fall. Seek out some cheerful, snugged-in types. The way they deal with the "Februaries" just might be contagious.

W H I L E a recent winter storm raged outside, I spent a peaceful afternoon reading about day lilies. This was unplanned. It was one of those delightful experiences of living, where once a word or topic surfaces, it seems to keep popping up again and again.

In filing some papers I came across a notation, "In *Little Women* their garden was planted with old-fashioned flowers. What kind of flowers were old-fashioned during the Civil War?" While this question was bouncing about in my head, I picked up an April 1971 issue of *Horticulture* with an article "Flowers of the Colonial Days." The author, Rudy J. Favretti, stated that day lilies were a popular perennial in the 18th century for the same reasons they're grown today— they will grow in sun or shade and in poor soil as well as good. These old-fashioned plants, having escaped cultivation, now beautify our roadsides.

Interesting. But I continued puttering about, putting things away. However, before replacing one book about the adventures and misadventures of two women trying to create order and beauty on a long-neglected New England farm, I browsed a bit. And almost at once—began to read about their attempts to root out masses of overgrown day lilies.

Not having established a compost heap, they tossed the excess clumps over the fences. The next year the fields were aglow with orange blossoms and—with no human aid—they continued to bloom year after year. These women decided that any plant which was that easy to raise to beautify their country acres was worth investigating, and they purchased and planted new varieties.

While shoveling out the mailbox again, lifting away the generous contributions of the town plow, I studied the snowbanks under which my day lilies rest. The plants will need dividing in the spring and perhaps that planting before the hemlocks would be more colorful if I investigated new varieties. And moved in some of the tall purple iris to grow with the lemon yellow lilies? In the gust-driven snow I could picture that garden in June.

The mail brought a letter from a friend who is just beginning to garden. "Are you a *Hemerocallis* fan? Have you seen what's being offered in the Wayside Gardens' catalog?" she wrote. "My grandmother used to have masses of day lilies around her outhouse, and we always called them privy flowers. Do you think they'd grow that luxuriantly on the septic drain here?"

That was when I settled down to read about day lilies. Because these plants have few pests, survive bitter cold winters, are long-lived and seldom need dividing or moving, they are a reliable perennial. Clumps of yellow *Hemerocallis flava* and the tawny orange *Hemerocallis fulva* can be found in most old gardens and in roadside patches. More than 22,000 varieties have been developed by plant breeders, so that it's difficult to locate a source from which to purchase specific day lilies popular just ten years ago. In an English novel (written by a gardener) I noted Royal Ensign and Bright Banner as varieties which might be a joy to behold in a Maine garden. But none of my catalogs list these. One aim in improving day lilies has been to increase the number of flowers produced on each stalk so that during the three to six weeks during which they bloom, the total effect will be more spectacular.

New varieties grow to different heights—from twelve inches to four feet. Fragrances, flower shapes and colors differ from the day lilies of the last century. But through all the breeding for improved varieties, day lilies retain their qualities which make them durable and adaptable perennials.

Clumps of day lilies have been flourishing along this country road without care or cultivation for all of the thirty-five years I've lived here. No other plants have crowded them out. When I divide my garden lilies this spring, I think I'll try planting some of the extras on the steep bank behind the house. They can serve to prevent erosion and to keep out noxious weeds. From the lawn chairs we can watch hummingbirds sipping *Hemerocallis* nectar.

The catalog photos of *Hemerocallis* are bright and cheerful. The descriptions promote the fact that day lilies bloom during the hottest part of the summer. Ideal reading during a raging winter storm.

WHEN I STARTED sorting out the navy blue and green items in my wardrobe, I found myself thinking of great-aunt Ella and her puddings. Whenever a serious illness occurred within the extended family during my childhood, this maiden lady arrived. Because Ella had no husband to wait upon and clean up after, it was assumed that she was free to come and help out.

I remember her as a little, bustling woman who expected children to have good manners. But mostly I remember the desserts she made while she was in charge of the kitchen. Before her bags were unpacked she'd say, "I think a nice healthy pudding will be good for supper." And it was good. And plentiful—more than we could eat.

So the next day great-aunt Ella, a thrifty soul, would add a little chocolate, an egg, some stale cake, and milk to stretch the leftover pudding for one more meal. Again it was good. But again it was plentiful and some was left over. Adding coconut, cornstarch and milk, Ella fixed that pudding into a dessert for one more meal. Fixed it generously.

In my memories of those days when great-aunt Ella helped out, we were still eating stretched-out, leftover puddings until the day she went off to cope with an emergency in the home of another relative.

Now here I am many decades later using that pudding technique with my wardrobe. By the time I find a jersey that is right to wear with a favorite pair of slacks, they're getting tacky so I start shopping for new slacks to match the jersey.

With the perspective of distance and hindsight, I can say that great-aunt Ella should have fed the leftover pudding to the cats and started anew. Maybe whipped up an apple pie or chocolate cake—something new and different. And looking at the navy blue and green items I'm sorting out, instead of adding to them, perhaps I need to pitch and try something new and different.

Fear of being destitute and dependent limited great-aunt Ella's living. When she was about to be married, she signed all her funds over to her husband-to-be who left town. Ella went back to work and saved only to have the bank close and never reopen. Making do and using up became lifetime habits.

My well-worn wardrobe is not important except that this served as a catalyst for remembering great-aunt Ella and her puddings—for seeing the habit of hanging on, a stuck-in-a-rut attitude. A new outfit in tones of heather and cream might lift my spirits—especially if all parts were new—but a more lasting satisfaction would come from trusting myself enough to change and move on to something new and different.

To change, to pitch out and make a fresh start. That thought lingered until it was joined by an idea I'd been juggling in my head for months. What would it be like to get rid of all the plants and over-grown shrubs around the house and plan a landscaping with some unity and balance?

Photographs of British gardens have delighted me for years. They don't foster envy because avenues of trimmed hedges require lots of hired trimmers and thus could not be copied here. But more illustrated gardening books are being published with colored photos of American gardens and, while some are large open-to-the-public acres of flowers and shrubs cared for by a staff, most of the pictures show what one or two ardent gardeners can do—have done. Evergreen hedges channel the eye to a distant view. Benches and low walls encourage resting to admire perennial borders and blossoming shrubs. Designed like a painting or a tapestry, the choices of flowers, walls, walks, and background trees have a relationship to one another.

Using liquid paper, I painted out all the shrubs and plants on a photograph of this house until it looked like the home was hauled in and settled on freshly bulldozed land. Again

I was reminded of great-aunt Ella. By throwing out (if only on paper) all the left-overs, possibilities for change were apparent. Dozens of ideas shown in the garden photos could be built in, planted in, here. But it took a blocking out of the old for me to see ways to move toward changes.

Letting go of the familiar—things, habits, or ideas—stirs uncertainty. Throwing out old pudding sounds easy so I'll keep that in mind while stretching to apply a letting-go and moving-on attitude to matters more important than desserts.

CHRISTIAN HERALD ASSOCIATION AND ITS MINISTRIES

CHRISTIAN HERALD ASSOCIATION, founded in 1878, publishes The Christian Herald Magazine, one of the leading interdenominational religious monthlies in America. Through its wide circulation, it brings inspiring articles and the latest news of religious developments to many families. From the magazine's pages came the initiative for CHRISTIAN HERALD CHILDREN and THE BOWERY MISSION, two individually supported not-for-profit corporations.

CHRISTIAN HERALD CHILDREN, established in 1894, is the name for a unique and dynamic ministry to disadvantaged children, offering hope and opportunities which would not otherwise be available for reasons of poverty and neglect. The goal is to develop each child's potential and to demonstrate Christian compassion and understanding to children in need.

Mont Lawn is a permanent camp located in Bushkill, Pennsylvania. It is the focal point of a ministry which provides a healthful "vacation with a purpose" to children who without it would be confined to the streets of the city. Up to 1000 children between the age of 7 and 11 come to Mont Lawn each year.

Christian Herald Children maintains year-round contact with children by means of a *City Youth Ministry.* Central to its philosophy is the belief that only through sustained relationships and demonstrated concern can individual lives be truly enriched. Special emphasis is on individual guidance, spiritual and family counseling and tutoring. This follow-up ministry to inner-city children culminates for many in financial assistance toward higher education and career counseling.

THE BOWERY MISSION, located at 227 Bowery, New York City, has since 1879 been reaching out to the lost men on the Bowery, offering them what could be their last chance to rebuild their lives. Every man is fed, clothed and ministered to. Countless numbers have entered the 90-day residential rehabilitation program at the Bowery Mission. A concentrated ministry of counseling, medical care, nutrition therapy, Bible study and Gospel services awakens a man to spiritual renewal within himself.

These ministries are supported solely by the voluntary contributions of individuals and by legacies and bequests. Contributions are tax deductible. Checks should be made out either to CHRISTIAN HERALD CHILDREN or to THE BOWERY MISSION.

Administrative Office: 40 Overlook Drive, Chappaqua, New York 10514
Telephone: (914) 769-9000